The Arts in Contemporary Healing

The Arts in Contemporary Healing

IRMA DOSAMANTES-BEAUDRY

Contributions in Psychology, Number 45
Paul Pedersen, Series Editor

Westport, Connecticut
London

Library of Congress Cataloging-in-Publication Data

Dosamantes-Beaudry, Irma.
  The arts in contemporary healing / Irma Dosamantes-Beaudry.
      p. cm. — (Contributions in psychology, ISSN 0736–2714 ; no. 45)
  Includes bibliographical references and index.
  ISBN 0–313–32198–1 (alk. paper)
    1. Arts—Therapeutic use.   I. Title.   II. Series.
  RC489.A72D67   2003
  615.8'5156—dc21   2003042854

British Library Cataloguing in Publication Data is available.

Library of Congress Catalog Card Number: 2003042854
ISBN: 0–313–32198–1
ISSN: 0736–2714

First published in 2003

Praeger Publishers, 88 Post Road West, Westport, CT 06881

An imprint of Greenwood Publishing Group, Inc.
www.praeger.com
Printed in the United States of America

∞™

The paper used in this book complies with the
Permanent Paper Standard issued by the National
Information Standards Organization (Z39.48–1984).

10 9 8 7 6 5 4 3 2 1

Copyright Acknowledgment

Contents

Series Foreword

The events of September 11, 2001, changed our world and our way of life in that world in remarkable ways. As we learn to cope with this new and dangerous situation, we depend more and more on streams of social support from spiritual and from psychological resources. This remarkable book is constructed on the confluence of psychotherapy, conceptions of self, perspectives of culture, and artistic expression as those streams of support come together to provide accurate assessment, meaningful understanding, and appropriate interventions for this brave new world.

In the words of the author: "This book introduces a model for coping with difficult catastrophic life transitions through the use of art-making as a process for healing. The book describes many of the individual and group healing functions that a creative, art-making process can serve for people who live in contemporary Western heterogeneous societies and lead modernist lifestyles. Such a process serves those who are forced to confront difficult life cycle changes or unexpected, cataclysmic events—times when rational, material and pragmatic solutions are insufficient to cope with the depth and breadth of emotional upheaval that such changes arouse."

I do not know of any other book in which the therapeutic perspective of art brings together the selves and the social systems around us as effectively as this volume. Life at its best is good art and those people who have discovered the secret of living artistic lives find more meaning and comfort by far than others. This book makes clear that art is a way of looking at ourselves and the world around us, which is in itself therapeutic, even when the artistic value may be obscure to those around us.

The artistic perspective engages harmony and balance with one another, giving meaning to symbols and meaning to identity. The artistic perspective is the cultural context in which we live, when rightly understood. This book is about the transformation of self and community by a creative art-making process that involves the exploration of the "in-between" psychological spaces as an agent for healing and an expression of therapy. The framework and structure of this book is filled with case examples to document and validate these assumptions about the therapeutic value of art.

This book presents a "developmental-relational arts-based model of healing." The author takes us on a psychological journey into the mysteries of our internal symbolic world. The focus is on subjective and emotional aspects of the self and the capacity of artistic expression to comfort, express, and clarify the shadow aspects of our self-experiences that are otherwise difficult to acknowledge. The author builds a solid foundation from the psychological theories and constructs of psychotherapy to demonstrate the therapeutic or healing that art-making processes make possible as a psychological journey into the mysteries of our internal symbolic world. As qualitative, subjective, and postmodern expression becomes more important in the field of psychotherapy, this book will be one of the leaders toward the new therapies for our brave new world.

As the 45th volume in the Greenwood Contributions in Psychology series, this book continues the tradition of exploring the cutting edge of applied psychology as a psychological journey into the mysteries of our internal symbolic world. Psychology is to this millennium what theology was in the previous millennium, an engine of change. The fields of psychology are going through rapid and radical alterations to match the changing society in which psychology is applied. Although there is some disagreement about the paradigm shift, there is almost universal agreement that profound changes are taking place in the field of psychology. The books in this series have been selected to help chart the progress of psychology as a discipline going through these changes. To the extent that the changes are being mediated by controversy, this series will be controversial. In any case, the emphasis is on applications of psychology to particular social problems. Some of the social problems addressed in the series have included identity issues, moral development, ethical thinking, self-representation, culturally competent therapy, and hostage trauma.

We hope that you share our enthusiasm for this book as you read through the pages of the new ideas it presents. You will not always agree with the author and may argue in your internal dialogues, which is itself your artistic privilege.

Paul Pedersen
University of Hawaii, Honolulu, Hawaii

Acknowledgments

Ultimately this book is a tribute to the resilience of the human spirit. However, I would personally like to dedicate it to three women, each of whom has played a significant and powerful role in shaping my view of life and the way I have chosen to live it. The first is my mother, Masha Dosamantes Badash, a strong and determined woman who had the courage to live in a foreign land, marry a foreigner, and raise two children as a single parent. She offered me many opportunities to resist and to push against her. Her legacy of being able to push against is what allowed me to become resilient and undaunted by whatever obstacles I have encountered during my life. The second is Dr. Alma Hawkins, who created the Dance Department at UCLA and was the first director of the Graduate Dance/Movement Therapy Program offered by this institution. She acted as a good teacher and mentor to me when I was a postdoctoral student at UCLA and later, when she passed the directorship of this program on to me. The third is Dr. Hedda Bolgar, my analyst, who taught me about the meaning of compassion, emotional containment, and tolerance for the paradoxes of life. I shall never forget what she said to me on the last day that we met as analyst and analysand, when I described to her how I had struggled that week to think of something to give her as parting gift, but that nothing material I possessed seemed to be as valuable as what she had given to me. She responded by saying that there was something I could give her. That was "to pass it on."

I want to thank all of the therapists and researchers whose work contributed significantly to the formulation of the arts-based developmental relational model that I have presented in this book. In particular, I wish to express my gratitude to all of the creative arts therapists, therapists, and artists whose healing work has been selected for citation in this book: Judith Francisca Baca, Jean Davis, Barbara Drucker, Janette Farrell Fenton, Craig Haen, Kenneth Brannon, Debra Kalmanowitz, Bobby Lloyd, Avigdor Klingman, Ronit Shalev, Abigail Pearlman, Mooli Lahad, Gaila Cattrell Lebherz, Craig Ng, Trudi Schoop, Peggy Mitchell, and Marion Scott, along with all of the clients, students, artist colleagues, performers, and staff who collaborated with them in their own creative work.

Last, I want to thank my husband, Walter A. Beaudry, for his unwavering support and sense of humor while I wrote this book.

Irma Dosamantes-Beaudry
University of California, Los Angeles

CHAPTER 1

Introduction

Within minutes of the sudden crash of two jumbo airliners into the Twin Towers of the World Trade Center in lower Manhattan on September 11, 2001, the skyscrapers pulverized and collapsed, generating an enormous tidal wave of thick gray dust that enveloped all in its wake. After the dust settled, all that remained at the site was a huge crater containing tons of debris and the remains of thousands of people. Similar horrific events occurred on the same day at the Pentagon in Arlington, Virginia, and in Shanksville, Pennsylvania. By the end of the day, over 3,000 lives had been lost. More lives were lost on this single day than had ever been lost on any day in the history of the United States.

THE ARTS IN TIMES OF CRISIS: FILLING THE VOID

Any violent attack aimed at defenseless victims that threatens the lives and well-being of human beings in unpredictable and uncertain ways can be called an act of terrorism (Medina, 2002, p. 39). As Americans awoke in stunned disbelief and as the enormity of their losses began to be recounted by the news media, they began to acknowledge the pain and vulnerability they were experiencing. The American popular arts community mobilized itself to respond to the emotional needs of a dazed nation in mourning. Americans needed to be comforted, they needed to experience solidarity and kinship with other victims, they needed to mourn their losses, and they needed to acknowledge the numerous heroic deeds that had been performed by those who found themselves at ground zero on that fateful day. The need to grieve so many loved ones assumed intense and overwhelming proportions. Numerous fund-raising concerts were spontaneously organized by artists locally and nationally. When words were inadequate to express the depth of despair, sorrow, pain, and outrage that Americans felt, they turned to the arts to fill the void; the arts became a vehicle through which to express their unspeakable emotions, to demonstrate their compassion for other people's pain, and ultimately to find some solace.

The terrorist attacks of September 11, 2001, generated large audiences for plays, concerts, and sporting events. Spectators were less interested in Mahler's Symphony No. 2 or Barry Bonds's home-run count than in being with other people who shared the same feelings of loss, fear, dislocation, and confusion (Marling, 2001). The sounds of somber, sad, soulful, despairing, angry, and patriotic songs filled the airways. An informal survey of radio requests for music following the attacks showed that older listeners preferred songs that dealt with patriotism and consolation, young ones called for songs of reassurance and heroism, and men in their late teens and early twenties requested fighting songs (Pareles, 2001a). Singing "My City of Ruins" at a benefit for the families of victims of the New York disaster, popular singer Bruce Springsteen commented that, though the song had been written prior to the events of September 11, "songs are funny, they go out to who needs them when they need them" (Pareles, 2001b, p. E5). Improvised memorials that included well-known poems as well as snatches of original verses were pinned alongside photos of the victims of the terrorist attacks. Former poet laureate of the United States Robert Pinsky attributed the power of poetry to move people emotionally to the fact that "poetry has an intimacy because it is in the reader's voice, in one person's breath" (Smith, 2001, p. E4).

In the aftermath of the explosions, two artists, Paul Myoda and Julian La Verdiere (2001), conceived a new art project they called *Phantom Towers*, which was featured on the cover of the *New York Times Magazine* of September 23, 2001. These artists imagined two powerful beams rising from a reflecting pool, refilling the void left by the Twin Towers with incandescence (see Photo 1.1). La Verdiere described the project in terms of the emotional response the towers elicited from them:

Those towers are like ghost limbs, we can feel them even though they're not there anymore. Not being doctors or licensed crane operators, we realized that the best thing we can do to help is an artistic gesture that might offer consolation or a sense of security or hope (Myoda & La Verdiere, 2001, p. 81).

The unexpected catastrophic events that took place on September 11, 2001, suddenly transformed the world into an unpredictable, hostile place to be. This is because when sudden and devastating events happen to people over which they have no advance warning and little control, they

Photo 1.1 *Phantom Towers* by Paul Myoda, Julian LaVerdiere, and *The New York Times Magazine*; original photograph by Fred R. Conrad/*The New York Times Company.* Copyright © 2001 *The New York Times.*

become disoriented until they can restore their emotional equilibrium and until they can arrive at a new understanding of what the changed world has become for them (Piaget, 1972).

This book introduces a model for coping with difficult catastrophic life transitions through the use of art-making as a process for healing. The book describes many of the individual and group healing functions of a creative, art-making process for people who live in contemporary Western heterogeneous societies and lead modernist lifestyles. Such a process serves those who are forced to confront difficult life cycle changes or unexpected, cataclysmic events; times when rational, material, and pragmatic solutions are insufficient to cope with the depth and breadth of emotional upheaval that such changes arouse.

A CONTEMPORARY, INTERDISCIPLINARY, DEVELOPMENTAL-RELATIONAL, ARTS-BASED MODEL OF HEALING

Toward the end of the twentieth century and continuing into the twenty-first century, contemporary Western notions regarding the causes of emotional problems and the care of persons experiencing them began to shift from single disciplinary solutions, such as the psychopathological and psychopharmaceutical solutions offered by the prevailing medical model, to more holistic, interdisciplinary approaches. Holistic approaches view physical, emotional, cognitive, psychosocial, and spiritual aspects of a person's well-being as interrelated and, therefore, important to consider as a whole.

For the most part, the traditional Western medical or disease model has focused on the prospect of curing the symptoms of illness rather than on maintaining or supporting wellness, growth, and development (Dolph, 1985). This model has tended to focus primarily upon the physical problems of the patient and has largely ignored the patient's emotional, psychological, cultural, and spiritual well-being. The practitioner who follows this model assumes the authoritarian position of knowing the single best diagnosis and cure for the patient's pathology, and the patient is expected to adopt a passive stance and to comply with the physician's directives (Cogswell, 1988).

In contrast, the practitioner who adopts a holistic or more comprehensive, interdisciplinary model of healing assumes the role of one among many consultants who ideally work collaboratively with one another and with each client to develop goals and strategies that will facilitate and maintain each client's wellness. The holistic healing model respects and supports the client's ability to use his or her available potential optimally while attempting to meet the demands and realities of everyday life. From this perspective, clients are viewed as active participants in their own healing process. They are encouraged to mobilize their own resources and to contribute actively toward optimizing the quality of their own lives (Schuster & Ashburn, 1992).

From a holistic perspective, healing differs from a cure because people can gain a sense of peace and wholeness even when they find themselves in the grip of an incurable illness. Increasingly, people who lead modernist Western lifestyles are coming to understand illness as the experience of fragmentation, and what they seek most from any healing process is to recover the sense of feeling well, integrated, and whole (Morris, 1998).

This book introduces a model for healing transitions through an art-making process that is embedded within the context of intimate as well as public psychosocial relationships. The model focuses on how members of Western societies who lead modernist lifestyles are making use of various arts modalities to cope with difficult developmental and external, or situational, transitions that they encounter during their lifetime. The model that is proposed in this book is interdisciplinary in nature. It does not rely solely upon the knowledge of a single discipline but borrows concepts derived from various Western disciplines such as psychoanalysis; clinical, social, and cognitive psychology; art history; anthropology; neuropsychoanalysis; and the practices of creative arts therapists and artists whose approaches to art-making share a healing intention. In this model, the psychosocial spheres of intimate and public relationships are treated as the sites where illusion, pretend playing, and creative art-making originate. In turn, the regenerative potential that these creative processes set into motion is conceived as capable of promoting self and communal transformation.

The clients whose case vignettes are presented in chapters 4 and 6 of this book vary with respect to age, physical well-being, level of emotional self-differentiation and coherence achieved, and types of developmental or catastrophic events they have experienced. Some have resided for a long time in state mental institutions or in community shelters and function on the margins of society. Others are terminally ill and reside in hospitals. Still others attend outpatient clinics or see practitioners in a private practice setting. There are some who are neither patients nor clients of the health and welfare system but who belong to social groups that have been oppressed and marginalized by dominant cultural groups. Then there are groups of so-called normal people who have been suddenly exposed to the abnormal conditions imposed by the outbreak of war. Many of these people functioned well until they came up against a major catastrophic event in their lives that overwhelmed them and suddenly thrust them into an involuntary state of regression.

All of the creative arts therapists and artists whose healing work is featured in this book make use of an art-making process to promote personal and communal transformation in the people with whom they work. Their practices differ with regard to the form and structure they take, depending upon the needs of the people with whom they work as well as the practitioners' views of the arts as healing modalities. Therapists who work with people who are confronting difficult developmental transitions focus on ways to facilitate the reconstruction and reorganization of each person's sense of self so that she or he can cope more effectively with the demands of the outside world. Therapists and artists who work with the oppressed and marginalized communities of our multicultural society seek to valorize the cultural identities and history of members of these groups in order to reduce intracultural and intercultural group conflict. All aspire to return the people with whom they work to a more balanced state of being. The practices of these healers seem to share and be based upon the following set of assumptions:

1. Physical, emotional, cognitive, psychosocial, and spiritual aspects of a person's well-being are interrelated. These domains of life can be negotiated within the intimate and public spheres of human psychosocial relationships (Bowlby, 1973; Geertz, 1973; Piaget, 1972; Stern, 1985; Taylor, 1994; Winnicott, 1982).

2. A person's sense of well-being is derived from the experience that all aspects of living are in harmony and in balance with one another (Katz, 1982).

3. Throughout the course of our lives, we encounter difficult external and developmental conditions that tend to be disruptive of life as we have known it (Bridges, 2001).

4. To restore our sense of balance and well-being, we need to find meaningful symbols and make appropriate physical and emotional accommodations to the conditions that we do encounter (Piaget, 1972; Winnicott, 1982).

5. The supportive object relationships that are facilitated by trained creative arts therapists and artists whose artwork process shares a healing intention help to set into motion a creative transformation that enhances a person's sense of self-mastery, self-agency, self-generativity, and self-cohesiveness, as well as her or his sense of belonging and relatedness with others (Bonny, 1997; Dosamantes-Beaudry, 1997; Landy, 1997: Lerner, 1997, McNiff, 1997).

6. The successful negotiation of all three phases that comprise the transition process allows one to find new symbolic meaning, new ways of being, and new, more effective ways of relating to one's self and others (Bridges, 2001; Dosamantes-Beaudry, 1998).

Transitions and the Generation of Cognitive Dissonance

External transitions are set into motion whenever sudden and unexpected events (e.g., natural catastrophes, wars, terrorist attacks, or the unexpected and violent loss of loved ones) trigger intense and immediate changes in our lives. Developmental transitions are set into motion by gradual life cycle changes (e.g., the gradual descent into a state of autism that a person who is labeled schizophrenic by psychiatrists undergoes over time, or a normal adolescent's search for his or her own distinctive identity). Although developmental transitions seem to offer one the opportunity to become more differentiated, mature, and whole, external transitions allow those who have been exposed to the same or similar catastrophic event to bond together and to develop a sense of *communitas* with one another, where the usual differentiation between people based on role, gender, race, and class gives way to a more basic open relatedness (Turner, 1969).

When confronting catastrophic events, how do we begin to make sense of the cognitive dissonance such events trigger? According to Piaget's

(1972) constructivist theory of cognitive development, people adapt to their environment by making use of two complementary cognitive processes, assimilation and accommodation. Assimilation involves the incorporation of new knowledge into already-existing cognitive structures or schemes. Accommodation entails the modification of existing cognitive structures or schemes in order to incorporate new knowledge. All transitions that necessitate an accommodation to major external and developmental life changes always involve both of these cognitive processes (Flavell, 1968; Piaget, 1972).

Although Piaget (1972) maintained that an individual's motivation for cognitive growth stemmed from a drive to achieve cognitive equilibrium, he also held that all cognitive growth is initially spurred on by the experience of conflict or a state of cognitive disequilibrium. Conflict is experienced whenever the person becomes aware that a discrepancy exists between her or his view of the world and the view that is shared consensually by others. The person resolves the conflict experienced through the processes of accommodation and assimilation, which facilitate his or her return to a state of cognitive equilibrium.

Negotiating Transitions through Creative Arts Therapies

The interdisciplinary, developmental-relational conceptual framework adopted in this book has much to contribute to our understanding of the various ways in which our emotional stability can be lost and restored within the context of our intimate and public relationships. It is within the context of these relationships that we learn to create illusion, to play, to express ourselves artistically, and to acquire the cognitive and emotional skills that contribute to a more differentiated and coherent sense of our selves and others, and to our development of resilience, which serves us well during times of crisis.

The transformation of self and community is set into motion by a creative art-making process that involves the exploration of the "in-between" psychological space, which Winnicott (1982) has referred to as "potential space" (p. 126). How an art-making process can become an agent for healing will be illustrated through several case-study vignettes drawn from the author's dance/movement therapy practice and from the practices of other creative arts therapists who use different arts modalities, as well as from the work of several artists whose artwork shares a healing intention with that of creative arts therapists.

CONTENT OF BOOK CHAPTERS TO FOLLOW

The concept of regression-reintegration as a key or core process concept underlying all healing transitions is introduced in chapter 2 (Koestler,

1977). Regression is the ability to maintain contact with early bodily self-states, types of object relationships, and modes of thinking (Knafo, 2002). This process is set into motion by a shift in state of consciousness from an active to a receptive state. When we function within a receptive state, we temporarily disengage from the realm of conscious, consensual reality and move into the realm of preconscious, illusory reality, where contact with less conscious aspects of our self-experience can be made. While in a receptive state, we are able to perceive disavowed "shadow" aspects of ourselves that we ordinarily find difficult to acknowledge and to accept when functioning within an alert, active state of consciousness.

Chapter 2 offers support for the notion that the successful negotiation of difficult developmental and external transitions requires our return to earlier modes of perceiving, thinking, and relating through pretend play with objects that we derive from our internal symbolic world. Such playful interactions lead to the creation of metaphors that, in turn, allow us to perceive problematic situations we are working on in fresh, novel ways. The mediation of difficult developmental and external life transitions is illustrated through several case vignettes.

Chapter 3 provides the developmental component of the theoretical framework adopted in this book. This chapter describes the significant contribution made by our early intimate psychosocial relationships to the development of our creative potential and our capacity for self-generativity and empathy. In this chapter, the Western family unit is presented as a crucible within which children come to acquire the basic social and creative skills that they depend upon throughout their lives. A critical relationship exists between the kinds of identifications and attachments children forge early in life and their subsequent capacity to adequately meet their society's expectations for age-appropriate behavior and comportment. The quality of care given by a family and a community to their children appears to predict their resilience to traumatic stress (Goleman, 1995).

Children who are able to establish synchronous, mutually gratifying relationships with their caregivers are optimally positioned to create gratifying illusory objects that can sustain them subsequently during times of crisis (Ainsworth, Blehar, Waters, & Wall, 1978). The process of illusory object-making begins in toddlerhood with the creation of the first transitional object; this process becomes the prototype for all future human creative activity (Winnicott, 1982). Later, the idealized relationship that an adult person is able to establish with a "wise and charismatic therapist" represents a special case of the idealized relationship that was initially forged during childhood with his or her primary caregivers.

As children leave their family of origin and venture out into the public sphere of psychosocial relationships, they continue to manipulate and play with concrete objects that they imbue with symbolic meaning, initially alone in a solitary way, and later in collaborative play with other children (Hurlock, 1978). In adulthood, individuals continue to relate to objects they find in their environment or conjure up from their imagination and to invest them with the magic of illusion in increasingly abstract ways that not only gratify their private personal needs and motives, but also bolster their social standing within the social groups to which they belong.

Chapter 3 introduces the field of creative arts therapies, the social conditions that facilitate our capacity for creativity and self-generativity, and the three modes of knowing that form the bases for all human artistic forms of expression. Nonverbal modes of experience and expression are cited as being particularly critical in the acquisition of the intrapersonal and interpersonal kinds of human intelligences because they make a more differentiated sense of self and a more nuanced way of relating to others possible.

Chapter 4 introduces the importance of object relationships in our lives and the personal one-to-one developmental-relational approach to arts-based healing adopted by many creative arts therapists in their work with clients who must negotiate the most difficult kind of developmental transition of all, that of self-regeneration. Several case vignettes illustrate the transformative process that several clients underwent when they became actively engaged in creating the three kinds of object relationships: (a) the subjective relationship they developed with the concrete objects they selected from their environment or derived from their own imagination, (b) the intersubjective relationship they co-constructed in collaboration with their therapist, and (c) the interpersonal relationship they forged with their therapist or with members of the creative arts therapies group to which they belonged.

The subjective relationship that clients of creative arts therapies create with the material or imaginary objects they conjure up from their own experience and imagination puts them in touch with less conscious, wish-fulfilling aspects of their own internal symbolic world. The evolving intersubjective relationship they establish with their therapist allows them to internalize functional aspects of their therapist that they need but lack at the outset of therapy. The unfolding interpersonal relationship that clients establish with others allows them to see themselves mirrored through other people's eyes. The feedback they receive from others about their character or behavior puts them in touch with the world of consensually validated reality.

Over time, these three kinds of relationships help to facilitate clients' internalization of critical psychological functions that they need in order to function more effectively in the world. The self-regeneration that a person undergoes as a result of a healing art-making process makes its presence known in the form of newly acquired capacities: (a) the capacity to organize one's subjective self-experience into a more coherent whole,

(b) the capacity to soothe one's self when alone, (c) the capacity to tolerate and regulate disruptive emotions better, (d) the capacity to modulate the expression of one's impulses better, (e) the capacity to be more flexible and spontaneous in one's expressive behavior, (f) the capacity to reclaim negative or shadow aspects of one's self-experience, and (g) the capacity to establish more benign and empathic social relationships with others whom one cares about.

Chapter 5 explores the contribution that public relationships make to our sense of belonging and to the development of our sense of *communitas*, which are of particular value when coping with difficult external transitions. This chapter stresses the fact that all healing practices developed within a particular culture, are culture specific, and cannot simply be appropriated and put on like an overcoat by members of another culture, because one's cultural worldview determines the parameters of the aesthetic norms and healing practices one is likely to embrace. This chapter provides some examples of the ways that different Western cultural groups have used art symbols to mediate their social standing during a particular moment in time. Because contemporary Western societies have compartmentalized and institutionalized many critical aspects of living, people who live in these societies often find it difficult to cope effectively with external and developmental life transitions.

Chapter 6 describes the work of several creative arts therapists and renowned artists who have adopted an interpersonal group or community approach to healing external transitions through an art-making process. The interpersonal relationships that members of these groups were able to establish with one another and the subjective relationships they were able to forge with the concrete objects they created collaboratively to bolster their sense of connectedness to one another and to reduce various kinds of conflict that arose among them. Through their active participation in these art-making groups, members learned to (a) overcome the social barriers that they initially brought with them to the group (e.g., barriers presented by differences in language spoken or social roles assumed in the outside world), (b) create meaningful rituals that helped them to celebrate the passing of a societally stigmatized life cycle, (c) create symbols that acknowledged their cultural identities and cultural histories, (d) restore hope among war refugees whose lives had been ravaged by war, (e) create international public artworks that inspire the peaceful resolution of global conflict, and (f) create public artworks to help remember collectively made sacrifices in order to complete the mourning process associated with national losses.

Chapter 7 recapitulates the key conceptual and practice process elements encompassed by the developmental-relational arts-based model of healing introduced in this book. This chapter concludes with several recommendations that are intended to help ensure the survival of the art-making process as a viable healing resource for people living in het-erogeneous, contemporary societies who are likely to confront an ever-increasing number of developmental and external transitions in the future.

ABOUT THE AUTHOR

As I began to write this book, I found myself reflecting upon some of the more difficult transitions that I have had to confront during my life, and one instantly came to mind. This is probably because it was the first time that I faced a major challenge in my life—that of leaving my home of birth and migrating to a foreign land against my will. By being able to re-create a new sense of home, where I could unravel the meaning that the metaphor of homelessness held for me through a language that I un-derstood, I was able to grieve the deep sense of loss that I felt and begin to create a new vision of home. When I began to create dances about this traumatic experience, I had an opportunity to discover the importance of the healing power of dance, which ultimately transformed the course of my life.

I was born and reared in Mexico City. My father was a well-known Mexican lithographer and painter and my mother was an American folk singer and concert performer. When I was 10 years old, my parents de-cided to divorce. Without consulting either my brother or me, my mother decided to return to her home of birth, New York City, following her divorce. As a consequence of what appeared to me to be a rather selfish and arbitrary decision, my brother and I were abruptly uprooted from our home of birth and familiar surroundings, and our relationships with our father and childhood friends were permanently severed. This forced mi-gration and the loss of all that was dear to me left me feeling empty, rootless, angry, isolated, and depressed.

During our new family's adjustment to our new homeland, my mother noticed that the deeply depressed state I was in did not subside. Then, one day, she came upon what she considered to be an ingenious solution to my problem. While we were attending a modern dance concert to-gether, she noticed that I temporarily sparked up. At the conclusion of the concert, she asked me whether I would be interested in taking dance classes from the same dancers whose performance we had just watched. I readily consented.

Students who were enrolled in modern dance classes with Alwin Ni-kolais and Murray Louis at the Henry Street Settlement House in New York City during the fifties were trained in a group with same-age peers. Besides being thoroughly trained in the movement techniques of modern dance, we were also encouraged to improvise and to create dances based upon our own life experiences and imagination. Through the creation of such dances, I gradually found a way to communicate about things that

I could not otherwise express verbally in Spanish or English. The central theme of the dances I created dealt with the pain of leaving behind all that I had cared about. At the conclusion of this profound grieving transition process, my optimism and liveliness returned. I felt grateful to have found a new home where I felt understood, and where I could express what I had experienced in imaginative and inventive ways that made me feel understood and whole.

When I look back upon the path that my professional career has taken, I am struck by the profound effect this particular transition had in shaping my character as well as my career choices, because from that time forward both dance and psychology became two inexorably intertwined interests in my life.

The subsequent training I obtained in dance, psychology, dance/movement therapy, and psychoanalysis led me to pursue several professional careers as a dance therapist, psychotherapist, psychoanalyst, university professor, and program director (I directed the Graduate Dance/Movement Therapy Program at the University of California, Los Angeles for 22 years). My interests in dance and psychology have also been reflected in the written work I have produced and in the professional service I have rendered to my fields as President of the American Dance Therapy Association in 1980, President of the American Association for the Study of Mental Imagery in 1982, and five years as Editor-in-Chief of the *Arts in Psychotherapy Journal* published by Elsevier Sciences Press.

The knowledge and experience I have acquired as a practitioner and teacher of contemporary Western arts healing practices and the broad perspective I have gained through my years of service as Editor-in-Chief of the *Arts in Psychotherapy Journal* initially fueled my desire to write this book several years ago. Following the catastrophic events of September 11, 2001, my resolve to complete it was strengthened. In writing this book, I wanted to provide a holistic and developmental-relational accounting for how a healing art-making process can help Western people who lead modernist lifestyles mediate difficult life transitions.

Csikszentmihalyi (1990) has observed that the patterns of a person's goal-oriented behavior coalesce later in life into a theme that gives it form and meaning. He found that people whose life themes were based upon personal experience and an awareness and exercise of choice shared several personality characteristics: (a) in most instances, their life themes were a reaction to a great personal hurt they suffered early in life, (b) they subsequently became involved in a search for the purpose and meaning of their suffering, and gradually came to regard their suffering as a possible challenge, (c) they developed the necessary skills with which to confront the challenge, and (d) they discovered and formed solutions to the challenge. Still later, they developed the desire to share their insights with others in more altruistic ways (p. 231). For me, the completion of this book both confirms and affirms the presence of this pattern within my own life.

REFERENCES

Ainsworth, M. D. S., Blehar, M. C., Waters, E., & Wall, S. (1978). *Patterns of attachment: Observations in the strange situation and at home.* Hillsdale, NJ: Erlbaum.

Bonny, H. L. (1997). The state of the art of music therapy. *Arts in Psychotherapy Journal, 24* (1), 65–73.

Bowlby, J. M. (1973). *Attachment and loss.* New York: Basic Books.

Bridges, W. (2001). *The way of transition: Embracing life's most difficult moments.* Cambridge, MA: Perseus Publishing.

Cogswell, B. E. (1988). The walking patient and the revolt of the client: Impetus to develop new models of physician-patient roles. In S. K. Steinmentz (Ed.), *Family and support systems across the life-span* (pp. 243–256). New York: Plenum Press.

Csikszentmihalyi, M. (1990). *Flow: The psychology of optimal experience.* New York: Harper & Row.

Dolph, C. D. (1985). Holistic health and therapy. In D. G. Benner (Ed.), *Baker encyclopedia of psychology* (pp. 516–518). Grand Rapids, MI: Baker Book House.

Dosamantes-Beaudry, I. (1997). Reconfiguring identity. *Arts in Psychotherapy Journal, 24* (1), 51–57.

Dosamantes-Beaudry, I. (1998). Regression-reintegration: Central psychodynamic principle in rituals of transition. *Arts in Psychotherapy Journal, 25* (2), 79–84.

Flavell, H. J. (1968). *The developmental psychology of Jean Piaget.* Princeton, NJ: Van Nostrand.

Geertz, C. (1973). *The interpretation of cultures.* New York: Basic Books.

Goleman, D. (1995). *Emotional intelligence.* New York: Bantam Books.

Hurlock, E. B. (1978). *Child development* (6th ed.). New York: McGraw Hill.

Katz, E. (1982). *Boiling energy.* Cambridge, MA: Harvard University Press.

Knafo, D. (2002). Reviewing Kris's concept of regression in the service of the ego in art. *Psychoanalytic Psychology, 19* (1), 24–29.

Koestler, A. (1977). In W. Anderson (Ed.), *Therapy and the arts* (pp. 3–10).

Landy, R. (1997). Introduction to special issue on the state of the arts. *Arts in Psychotherapy Journal, 24* (1), 3–4.

Lerner, A. (1997). A look at poetry therapy. *Arts in Psychotherapy Journal, 24* (1), 81–89.

Marling, K. A. (2001, October 14). Salve for a wounded people. *The New York Times, Arts & Leisure Section,* pp. 1, 39.

McNiff, S. (1997). Art therapy: A spectrum of partnerships. *Arts in Psychotherapy Journal, 24* (1), 37–44.

Medina, G. S. (2002). Focus: The mind of the fundamentalist/terrorist. Terrorism and psychoanalysis. *Newsletter of the International Psychoanalytic Association, 11* (1), 38–39.

Morris, D. B. (1998). *Illness and culture.* Berkeley, CA: University of California Press.

Myoda, P., & La Verdiere, J. (2001, September 23). Filling the void. *The New York Times Magazine,* pp. 80–81.

Pareles, J. (2001a, October 1). Pop anthem or classic couplet to sustain a weary soul. *The New York Times, The Living Arts Section,* pp. E1, E3.

Pareles, J. (2001b, October 22). Pop's icons grapple with new role. *The New York Times, The Living Arts Section,* pp. E1, E5.

Piaget, J. (1972). *Play, dreams and imitation in childhood.* New York: Norton.

Schuster, C. S., & Ashburn, S. S. (1992). *The process of human development: A holistic life-span approach* (3rd ed.). Philadelphia: JB Lippincott.

Smith, D. (2001, October 1). Pop anthem or classic couplet to sustain a weary soul. *The New York Times, The Living Arts Section,* pp. E1, E4.

Stern, D. N. (1985). *The interpersonal world of infants.* New York: Basic Books.

Taylor, C. (1994). The politics of recognition. In D. T. Goldberg (Ed.), *Multiculturalism: A critical reader* (pp. 75–106). Malden, MA: Blackwell Publishers.

Turner, V. W. (1969). *The ritual process.* Chicago: Aldine.

Winnicott, D. W. (1982). *Playing and reality.* New York: Penguin Books.

CHAPTER 2

Transitions and the Regression-Reintegration Process

The negotiation of difficult life transitions always entails a degree of regression or a return to an earlier mode of perceiving, behaving, and relating. Regression can be defined as the ability to maintain contact with early bodily self-states, types of object relationships, and modes of thinking (Knafo, 2002). Koestler (1977) considered our capacity to regress and to reintegrate to be a major step in the evolution of human consciousness. He maintained that within the context of a facilitative environment, regression to an earlier level of emotional development is always followed by a new and creative reorganization of the self, within the parameters permitted by the person's own particular culture. He used the French proverb *reculer pour mieux sauter*, "running backward in order to get a better jump," to underscore the fact that, to create a renewed sense of self, a person must undergo one or more regressions (p. 4).

Tribal societies that follow oral traditions have incorporated the theme of regression-reintegration in the initiation rites and healing rituals that they have practiced for thousands of years (Eliade, 1995; Halifax, 1982; Katz, 1982). In these rituals, the neophyte faces a crisis situation and, with support from a wise person from the community, is transported to another world (regression). There, through sacrifice or struggle, she or he acquires critical sacred knowledge (gathered while in an altered, receptive state of consciousness) and finally returns home, a more enlightened and transformed being, someone whom society regards as a more socially mature person (reintegration).

Van Gennep (1960) conceived of the process involved in initiation rites in terms of three phases:

1. Separation. This phase is characterized by the person's detachment from an earlier fixed state.

2. Minimal. In this phase the person enters the status of a neophyte. This state is characterized by ambiguity and a lack of self-definition.

3. Aggregrate. During this phase, the person returns home as a renewed and wiser person.

For most adults who live in contemporary Western heterogeneous societies and who follow modernist lifestyles, the sacrificial aspects of ancient rituals no longer have any meaning and are no longer being concretely and vividly enacted as they are among traditional tribal communities, but instead have become interiorized and have come to be viewed as internal experiences and events. Regressive experiences previously enacted within societally sanctioned rituals, myths, and fairy tales are now being rediscovered and understood in psychological terms as the story of one's desires and one's life experiences (Campbell, 1956; Janus, 1990).

In working with persons who have been traumatized by catastrophic events, it is valuable to track the origins, development, and maintenance of the full range of personal and cultural identifications they have internalized and the attachment styles they have formed because these identifications and attachments contribute significantly to how they react under extreme stress. A *developmental perspective* encompasses a person's entire life history, including the traumatic experiences that she or he has lived through. The adoption of a developmental perspective is helpful because it moves health and welfare practitioners beyond a model of healing that focuses only on the alleviation of or the lifting of symptoms by helping both the client and the practitioner understand the full range of psychodynamic and social variables that interact and affect the client's responses to a given traumatic event. In Western, modern, multicultural societies, developmental transitions now refer to how one comprehends and negotiates the demands made by society as one crosses from one developmental stage to the next, spanning one's entire life. Each developmental stage poses different kinds of psychosocial challenges that the person must successfully negotiate:

During infancy, children are capable of attending and influencing their environment, but their continued growth is contingent upon their caregiver's consistent and effective responses to their needs. If a mutually gratifying relationship evolves between infant and caregiver, children are able to forge a meaningful, positive emotional relationship with at least one adult, to acquire a core sense of self, and to develop the beginnings of interpersonal communication skills. The temporary absence of their primary caregiver provides children with a challenge and an opportunity to engage in the first creative act of their lives, the creation of a transitional object (Winnicott, 1982). (More is said about the significance of this event for the future creative capacity of children in chapter 3).

During toddlerhood, children's curiosity and capacity to engage in make-believe play expands. They begin to engage in wish-fulfilling fantasies and to dramatically enact adult social roles while their parents simultaneously attempt to guide or pressure them into compliance with what they consider to be culturally acceptable behavior (Bettelheim, 1989).

The school years are the primary years of acculturation. During this time, children learn to identify with their gender, ethnic, racial, and other cultural groups. Their circle of significant others begins to expand beyond the borders of their own family of origin. Children may meet some teachers whose values differ significantly from those of their parents. They also encounter many opportunities to cooperate as well as to compete with their peers. During adolescence, youth begin to assume adult social roles and responsibilities, though the fact that many youth remain financially dependent upon their parents while pursuing educational goals beyond high school often makes the completion of this task an ambivalent one for parents and adolescents. During adolescence, teens begins to forge a unique identity of their own (Erikson, 1968). For some, this challenge may cause them to revisit toddlerhood, an earlier time when they first experienced the vulnerability of separating physically and psychologically from their family of origin (Mahler, Pine, & Bergman, 1975). Adolescents are thus afforded a second chance to rework unresolved issues pertaining to an earlier stage of the separation-individuation process.

Young adults face multiple decisions—marriage, career, children, social affiliations, financial planning—all of which significantly impact the quality of their future lives (Schuster & Ashburn, 1992). During middlescence, adults have an opportunity to reevaluate or consolidate life decisions they have made earlier. Middle-aged adults are sometimes referred to as the "sandwich generation" because their needs are often sandwiched in between those of their children, who are seeking increased independence, and those of their aging parents, who are facing the loss of their independence (Myers, 1988). If all goes well, the experience and knowledge gained by middle-aged adults gives them the confidence to face life with greater wisdom and equanimity. During senescence, adults are expected to find meaning in nonemployment activities, to reflect upon the lives they have led, and to come to terms with their own mortality (Schuster & Ashburn, 1992). Jung (1968) emphasized the importance of reconciling opposite aspects of one's personality, particularly during the second half of one's life, when the major quest of life becomes the integration of disparate elements and finding a balanced sense of wholeness.

Although the kinds of changes involved in these developmental transitions may sometimes be difficult, they are at least anticipated, and most of the time they occur gradually. In contrast, the kinds of changes that trigger an external transition are sudden and unexpected. The person is neither expecting these changes nor is prepared to cope with them (e.g., natural catastrophes, terrorist attacks, wars). The impact of external, sudden, unexpected changes is particularly pernicious when the changes involve violence and the loss of life because such experiences shatter a person's faith in the trustworthiness of people (Terr, 1990). In negotiating either type of transition (developmental or external), a person is compelled to undergo varying degrees of regression (Dosamantes-Beaudry, 1998; Janus, 1990).

THE NEED FOR FAITH AND HOPE DURING TIMES OF CRISIS

Following the catastrophic events of September 11, 2001, attendance at American churches and synagogues increased from 5 to 10 percent (Gibbs, 2001). The American Bible Society reported a 42 percent rise in the sales of Bibles compared with the same period during the previous year. A fresh brand of secular faith also emerged. Police and firefighters, who had previously been viewed as the face of public authority at the street level, now were bathed in a bright new light. They were idealized and publicly worshipped as heroes. They became the saviors of the hour.

For many Americans for whom organized religions offer little meaning or consolation during times of crisis, the art-making process itself has become imbued with a sense of the sacred because of its potential to serve as a bridge between ordinary, conscious, material reality and extraordinary, unconscious, imaginal reality. By shifting from an active to a receptive state of consciousness, people are able to make direct contact with primary-process sorts of experiences that have the power to alter their view of reality and to foster a sense of awe and reverence for the unknown. While in a receptive state, they are free to engage in pretend playing with objects and symbols they find in the outside world or they derive from their own imagination, and then to create novel metaphors about these illusory objects that help to transform their perceptions of themselves, others, and the world (Dosamantes-Alperson, 1979).

As Western health care professionals have become aware of the importance of the process of regression in restoring their clients' sense of balance, some have turned to the arts as media through which their clients can make direct contact with the less conscious, primary-process experience. Creative arts therapists are health care practitioners who are specifically trained in the therapeutic use of the arts. They are trained to facilitate the potential space that enables clients to engage in pretend playing with objects and symbols they find in their environment or derive from their own experience and imagination, and then work through the meaning that these less conscious modes of experience hold for them. (The emergence and development of the field of creative arts therapies in this country from the time of its inception during the 1960s to the present is traced in chapter 3).

THE ARTS IN THE NEGOTIATION OF CONTEMPORARY TRANSITIONS

Turner (1987) referred to rites of passage as rites of transition because they prepare a person to cross from one state of being to another. This shift in states of being in the world is illustrated by the following case of a white, middle-aged married woman with a family, who began the arduous journey of coming to terms with the external transition of losing her home to fire suddenly and unexpectedly.

Gaila was in her forties when the catastrophic event to be described took place. As a choreographer and dance teacher, she was able to successfully cope with this unexpected event through a transition process that made use of her own creative resources and preferred mode of expression, dance. Through the wise counsel and support she received from her therapist and a fire survivors group, she was able to transform her personal tragedy into a healing ritual that came to involve everyone in her community who also had experienced major losses to fire.

Gaila lived with her husband, an opera singer, and three teenaged daughters in a beautiful home in Laguna Hills, California. Suddenly one day, without warning, fires appeared out of nowhere and engulfed her entire hillside community. These fires spread very rapidly, ravaging her home and all of her worldly possessions. When the fires subsided, nothing was left standing. Although she and her family escaped with their lives, her home and all of its contents were destroyed. Her possessions, which included a baby grand piano and other instruments used by her husband, opera scores, family photographs, works of art, personal mementos, clothing, and furniture—many of which held precious memories and great emotional value for her and her family—were gone.

Gaila became so distraught over this catastrophic event in her life that she sought help from a therapist to help her overcome her deep distress and depression. She began to attend a group composed of fire survivors. Her therapist encouraged her to create a dance about her experience. As a dance teacher, Gaila choreographed *Fire Dance* for her students at the college where she taught and invited the members of her fire survivors group to watch her students' performance. When the survivors group members saw the dance, they were so deeply moved that they requested that she re-create the dance with them as the performers and invite their loved ones to the performance.

What had started out as an experiment in self-healing soon became a ritual performed by and for the entire community of fire survivors. The following is a brief description of the dance that she created:

Fire Dance begins as a pleasant, calm, and flowing movement exchange between the dancers; gradually they are overwhelmed by terror and panic as they become aware of the flames that surround them. All attempts to confront the fires seem fruitless. The fires consume all things in their wake (see Photo 2.1). Following the scourge of everything by the flames, a sense of calmness returns. The dancers gradually emerge from the ashened ground; standing tall and naked, they turn to face each other, silently taking in what is mirrored in each other's faces. Then, slowly they turn to face the audience as the dance concludes.

Photo 2.1   *Fire Dance,* by Gaila Cattrell Lebherz, M.A., DTR. Videotaped Performance, 1994.

When the dance was viewed by the loved ones of the performing fire survivors group, the event proved to be a healing experience for all who were present. The *Fire Dance* performance triggered a communal emotional catharsis that had each person present sharing his or her own personal story and grieving over the loss that each had endured.

The emotional impact that the successful negotiation of this external transition process generated prompted Gaila to seek and to complete training as a dance therapist (Dosamantes-Beaudry, 1998). Her story is reminiscent of the trial-by-fire initiation rites endured by shamans who become healers as a consequence of confronting an overwhelming life or death ordeal or as a result of a life-threatening illness (Eliade, 1995; Halifax, 1982; Stewart, 2000).

For many disaster survivors as well as firsthand and secondhand observers, particularly when the catastrophic event experienced or witnessed involves violence or the loss of life, obtaining support from others who have been exposed to the same event may not be sufficient to allow them to function effectively in their lives. Individuals who have been deeply traumatized by cataclysmic events may manifest several characteristic behaviors that psychiatrists associate with a condition they refer to as posttraumatic stress disorder: a state of increased arousal, repeated reexperience of the traumatic event, persistent avoidance of stimuli associated with the event, and the numbing of general responsiveness (American Psychiatric Association, 1994). A healing, creative art-making process that focuses upon the needs of the traumatized person allows her or him to confront avoided stimuli and to synthesize physiological, affective, cognitive, and spiritual responses to the dreaded event.

One reason that creative arts therapies are effective in dealing with traumatized persons is that this form of therapy focuses on facilitating their accessibility to the very sensory, bodily-felt emotional reactions and images that traumatized persons tend to dissociate from and to repress. Creative arts therapies broach traumatic experiences through the use of various arts media. They encourage the emergence of spontaneous, pretend play and an awareness of the ironic and the humorous in life. The relaxed, accepting atmosphere that creative arts therapists facilitate gives clients an opportunity to vent denied or unexpressed emotions and an opportunity to reintegrate the emotional meaning that a catastrophic event currently holds for them in their lives.

VOLUNTARY AND INVOLUNTARY REGRESSION

All transitions involve some degree of regression, which implies a willingness to temporarily return to earlier, primary modes of perceiving and thinking. While in a regressed state, the experiential boundaries that exist between consensually accepted reality and imaginal, subjective reality become relaxed and sometimes become fused (Kubie, 1961). Benign or voluntary regression occurs whenever a person elects to engage in a creative activity that temporarily immerses him or her in a receptive, primary-process state of being; when the psychological journey has been completed, benign regression allows the person to return to the world of rational, consensual reality. While under the influence of a benign regression, most persons are able to retain their capacity for self-reflection and some emotional distance from their experience. Knafo (2002) refers to this type of regression as adaptive regression. I refer to this type of regression as benign regression.

When Kris (1952) introduced the concept of regression in the service of the ego, he wanted to draw a contrast between the benign or adaptive form of regression and the form of regression that results when a person becomes overwhelmed by a traumatic event. Recently, Sandler and Sandler (1994) noted that, although a benign or adaptive regression involves a temporary loss of functional autonomy, a structural regression results in the permanent impairment of the structural intactness of a person's sense of self.

When individuals undergo an involuntary or structural regression, the boundaries between their outer consensual reality and their own subjective reality become blurred and fused. They remain mired in a state of regression over which they have little control and cannot avoid. They communicate primarily through metaphors encoded and expressed in enactive, imagistic modes and concrete metaphoric language rather than the syntactical language of secondary-process thinking. The subjective experience of structurally regressed persons is dominated by primary-process thinking; hallucinatory, wish-fulfilling fantasies; raw, untamed instincts; fusion with the external world; and the absence of an observing ego (Knafo, 2002).

Others who may be cut off from a conscious awareness of these modes of experience are likely to feel threatened by the behavior of structurally regressed persons and to stigmatize them for it (Laing, 1967, 1969; Price & Denner, 1973; Szasz, 1973). Yet, persons who are structurally regressed must rely upon the presence of at least one caring adult to accompany them through their regressive journey and their return to ordinary reality. Their companion on such a journey must be someone who has their best interests at heart, is familiar with altered states of being, does not fear becoming overwhelmed or getting lost in these states, can assist them in processing the symbolic meaning of their journey, and can help them return safely to the experiential realm of ordinary reality.

The following case vignettes involve three women named Mary. Each of these women was stuck in a state of emotional isolation and involuntary regression. Their sole means of conveying how they felt in this state of involuntary regression was through their own bodily-felt experience and bodily products. The following case vignettes describe how these women came to use dance/movement and painting as media through which to break through their isolation and to reach out to an available caring adult in order to negotiate the most difficult developmental transition of all, that of self-generation or self-reconstruction.

THE THREE MARYS

Mary One

Trudi Schoop, a pioneer in the field of dance/movement therapy, was hired by Camarillo State Hospital in California during the 1960s to work as a dance therapist with the wards of this large psychiatric institution (Schoop & Mitchell, 1974). One day Trudi noticed Mary, a young black woman who had not spoken since being admitted to the hospital some three years earlier. Although Mary was mute, she did engage in a kind of restless, angry pacing that gave Trudi the impression of someone who was "angrily but methodically measuring the fifty-foot distance between the walls" (p. 73).

Initially, Trudi joined Mary by attempting to match Mary's moods and actions. Gradually, Trudi introduced variations in ways of pacing and sometimes she would extend a hand toward Mary. Although Mary began to vary her ways of pacing and to emulate the pattern variations introduced by Trudi, she remained mute.

Then one day, after a particularly exhausting session involving pacings that included jumps and hops, Trudi sank wearily into the floor, exclaiming, "You know, Mary, I really feel terribly lonesome." Finally, after many months of muteness, Mary broke her silence and asked, "You feel lonesome, Trudi?" (Schoop & Mitchell, 1974, p. 75). Once Mary's range of motion had widened and she could engage in verbal dialogues with others, Trudi felt that Mary was ready to join others like her in group sessions.

Mary Two

In 1965, R. D. Laing, a British psychiatrist, established Kingsley Hall, a residential healing community in the east end of London. Instead of the examination, diagnosis, and medication, which are the hallmarks of Western psychiatric treatment, Laing (1967, 1969) offered to those who were about to undergo a "mental breakdown" an initiation ceremonial through which the person would be guided to regress with full social encouragement and sanction from the community.

The community of Kingsley Hall was deliberately set up without the caste system that generally exists within psychiatric wards. The mental health care professionals who acted as caregivers also lived in the community. They were not accorded special privileges because of their social status. They made no attempt to distance themselves emotionally from the regressed residents nor did they stigmatize them because of their regressed state. Individuals contributed to the community in accordance with their capacity to do so. Decisions were reached by the consensus of the entire community.

A collaborative autobiographical accounting was written by Mary Barnes, a resident of Kingsley Hall who underwent the ordeal of a psychotic break and an involuntary regression with the help of another resident, psychiatrist Joseph Berke, who became her guide (Barnes & Berke, 1991). When Mary began to regress, she stopped eating solid foods and had to be fed milk from a bottle by other residents. She stopped talking and laid in bed for long periods of time. She describes her ordeal in the following way:

> Gradually I got more and more still. . . . My body did often seem apart. A leg or an arm could be on the other side of the room. Often it seemed I was floating and moving as if in fluid. . . . Although I lay as if in a stupor for most of the time, I was very aware of what was going on. Touch seemed to mean everything. By it I drew away or inwardly nearer. The wall behind me seemed hollowed into a great space into which I was going. Though, actually lying still,

curled up in my bed, it sometimes seemed I was on the other side of the room (Barnes & Berke, 1991, pp. 111–113).

As Mary began to cohere, she began to use her own feces to paint on the walls of her room. Then, one day, she showed up before Joseph Berke with her entire body covered in feces. When Joe saw her, he was shocked and repelled by her. But within a few moments he recovered, realizing that, unless he could accept her in all her despicableness, he would never again be able to work with another person who might be stuck in the same state that Mary was. Thus, he overcame his disgust of her and took her to the bathroom at Kingsley Hall and bathed her in the tub, as one would an infant (Barnes & Berke, 1991). When Mary became better integrated, she continued to paint with her fingers, but instead of using her own bodily products, she now turned to the use of oils as her painting medium.

Mary Three

During the early 1970s, I co-led several dance/movement therapy groups with a younger dance therapy intern. Together, we acted in the capacity of outside consultants at a local mental hospital in Los Angeles. While conducting a group session with several regressed adult women, Mary Three marched in flanked by two male attendants on either side of her. She had a wild look about her and she did not speak but only nodded assent or dissent to questions directed to her. When I asked her whether she wanted to join the group, she nodded no. One of the attendants interrupted her, stating that the psychiatrist in change of her ward "had ordered" that she be in the group. I told Mary that, although I could not override group assignments ordered by her primary physician, my cotherapist and I were in change of the movement studio space and therefore, while she was in the movement studio with us, she could choose to participate or not as she felt like it. At the time, I recall thinking that later I would have to confer with her psychiatrist to get his opinion about whether she could tolerate and benefit from being in the group and also whether the group could tolerate and benefit from her participation in the group. He replied that, in his opinion, she could and they could. However, this proved to be more problematic than he or I and my cotherapist could have anticipated.

Initially, Mary spent many dance/movement therapy sessions ensconced in one corner of the movement studio simply observing the goings-on. During this time, however, she did manage to make her presence known to everyone in a rather direct and disruptive way. When other group members moved or attended quietly to their own bodily-felt experience, she sighed loudly and frequently, letting everyone around her know that while she was present, she would not join in on any of the group's movement sessions. For their part, the group seemed perfectly willing to let her be. I thought at the time that, had she been in a group of better functioning adults, they might have asked her to leave the group, but the members of this group seemed to be more tolerant of behavior that better functioning people might have regarded as bizarre or annoying. I believe this was because they could identify with the rage that she expressed so blatantly and directly toward authority figures.

Then, one day when the group was working in dyads and exploring the experience of giving and receiving another person's weight, Mary left her corner perch, stood up, and decided to join the group. My cotherapist and I decided that I would work with Mary while she continued to attend and work with the rest of the group. Mary placed herself directly in front of me and then moved back to the opposite end of the room, from where she proceeded to lunge at me while moving at a fast pace and mustering all the force she could against me. Her sudden forceful lunge sent me sliding on my posterior across the room. I picked myself up and then told her, "that was fine; now it is my turn." I moved closer to her, and pressed and pushed forcefully against her. This pushing and pressing against one another, back and forth, continued until the group session ended.

In this group it had been customary to reserve time at the end of each session, so that any group member who cared to could verbally share any aspect of their movement experience with the group. After several group members had spoken, Mary decided to speak. The only statement she made was "I like Mexican tamales." Through her metaphoric use of language, Mary managed to convey that she liked me, because physically I happen to be a short, compact Mexican woman. From that point forward, Mary continued to attend the group until the time of her discharge to an outpatient facility.

What did all three Marys share in common? All of them were in a dire predicament. Their life space and choices over time had become extremely narrowed, inflexible, and limited. All three were stuck in a regressed, isolated state that psychiatrists label schizophrenic. In the case of Mary One, Trudi Schoop was able to communicate to Mary an acceptance of her as she was, through her willingness to follow her and to join her at a pace set by her. In the case of Mary Two, Joseph Berke was able to convey to Mary Barnes that he was willing to accept her at her worst and that, though her behavior disturbed him emotionally, he cared enough about her to overcome his disgust of her. I was able to convey to Mary Three that I would not coerce her into giving up her hard-won isolation and anger, and that her anger did not destroy me. Because each was shown respect by being granted a sense of control over her own destiny, each was able to break through her isolation and begin to relate emotionally to another human being.

(Chapter 4 features the work of several creative arts therapists who have made use of the regenerative potential of an art-making process to help voluntarily and involuntarily regressed clients cope with the most difficult developmental transition of all, that of self-regeneration.)

THE SHADOW: RECLAIMING ONE'S PROJECTIONS

When people are cut off from an opportunity to acknowledge and to work through all of the phases of the transition process, or when there are no wise or charismatic adults to guide them through their ordeal and through whatever obstacles they do encounter, their reactions are likely to take the form of unconscious enactments that are devoid of symbolic meaning. According to Meade (1995), when rites of passage disappear from conscious expression, they assume unconscious or semiconscious guises. Some of the social problems that we face today as a society can be attributed, in part, to our unconscious attempts to complete life cycle transitions that have been only partially completed and therefore lack substance and symbolic meaning for the participants.

For instance, the gang beatings and military hazings administered to some male initiates represent unconsciously enacted transition rites in which only the first two phases of the transition process have been concluded, but the third phase remains incomplete. When the last phase of a transition process is missed, initiates and other participants fail to find the deeper meaning of their enacted experience and to build a connection with like-minded souls. Similarly, drug addictions can be viewed as aborted attempts to achieve self-transformation that, rather than leading to self-renewal, remain blocked at the second phase of the transition process and instead continue to be repeatedly reenacted as a kind of narcotically induced sleep death.

Our society's dread over emotional disruption and loss of control tend to be manifested in all of the phases of the transition process. Because we fear the loss of control and our grasp on the only reality we have known, we may resist the first phase of the transition process, which entails letting go of our old accustomed ways. Because we associate diffused states with chaos and madness, we may resist the second phase of the transition process, which involves the relinquishment of control, the loss of well-defined boundaries, and the experience of vulnerability and emotional pain. Because we fear taking risks, being plunged into the abyss of the unknown, and the pain associated with making new symbolic connections, we may resist the third phase of the transition process.

Klinkenborg (2001) has observed that in the aftermath of the September 11, 2001, disasters, some entertainment sectors, namely, television and film industries, sheepishly sought to present only programming that offered consolation and inoffensive escapism, under the mistaken assumption that what we needed as a society was to avert our eyes from what we had watched in horror in order to protect our innocence from being further accosted. He argued that this was a false assumption and it did a disservice to the cultural function that artists serve best, that of daring to look at the world with an unflinching gaze and not being cowarded by unsavory realities. He argued that "the artist's job, however unseemly it may feel, will inevitably be to fracture this momentary mood, to lead us beyond what is merely safe and consoling" (p. 12).

Besides providing us with an opportunity to release pent up emotions and to find solace and comfort during times of crisis, the arts have the power to face us with those unpleasant realities about ourselves that we find difficult to acknowledge individually and collectively. These disavowed aspects of ourselves become reflected in what Jung (1968) referred to as our "shadow." The shadow disguises itself in our projections: when we react intensely to a trait in others but fail to see the trait in ourselves. The shadow lurks in our addictions that serve to deaden unpleasant emotions and to fill an invisible emptiness. The shadow blurts out in slips of the tongue. It erupts in humor, particularly in the cruel jokes that we deliver at another's expense (Zweig & Wolff, 1997).

We tend to project unloved aspects of ourselves to other individuals and groups. Keen (1991) has detected the presence of a collective shadow in the willingness of all cultures to engage in the process of "enemy-making" (p. 197). Zweig and Abrams (1991) contend that, no matter how repugnant this idea may be, we all seem to need enemies to serve as repositories for all behaviors and emotions that we are unable to collectively tolerate within ourselves:

At the level of nation, race, religion or other collective identity, we can witness enemy-making being enacted in mythic, dramatic, and often tragic proportions. . . . The greatest cruelties in human history have been carried out in the name of righteous causes, when the shadows of entire nations have been projected onto the face of an enemy, and thus an alien group can be made into a foe, a scapegoat, or an infidel (Zweig & Abrams, 1991, p. 195).

According to Meade (1995), when a culture fails to make real changes from the symbolic sacrifices that are enacted by a community and to derive new meaning from individual suffering, the quality of life decreases and the quantity of potential violence increases for everyone. Without a social environment that offers caring emotional containment, guidance, and meaning, the second chance for rebirth sought by ritual initiates and by those seeking self-transformation is aborted. When only the first two phases of the transition process are enacted and the meaning they contain is not processed, the end result is chaos and violence. The self-renewal and communal restoration of balance that characterizes the third phase remain unfulfilled. This means that healing happens only when all three phases of the transition process are effectively mediated and concluded.

The potential space created within a healing art-making process allows us to confront and reclaim aspects of ourselves that we fear, are ashamed of, feel disgusted by, and dread. Acknowledging these parts of ourselves allows us to gain a more realistic and less perfect sense of ourselves and to become more accepting and compassionate toward others. The process of reclaiming shadow aspects of ourselves means learning to read the messages encoded in the events of our daily lives in such a way that we

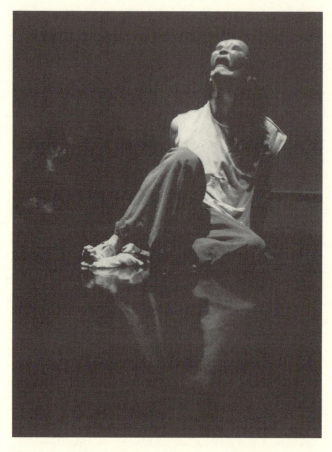

Photo 2.2   Craig Ng performing dance with Balinese mask in *Spirit Dances 5: Masks as Intermediaries*, conceived and directed by Marion Scott, Highways Performance Space, Los Angeles, October 12–14, 2002. Original photograph by Min Kim; copyright Min Kim.

gain consciousness. It involves taking responsibility for our feelings, actions, and thoughts instead of blaming others (Ogden, 1986). It entails deepening our awareness, opening up our hearts, abandoning our ideals of perfection, and learning to hold paradox (Zweig & Wolff, 1997).

In the dance performance *Spirit Dances 5: Masks as Intermediaries*, renowned American modern dance choreographer Marion Scott encouraged her dancers to work with a mask of their own choosing that held some attraction for them. Dancer Craig Ng chose to work with a Balinese mask that he was drawn to, a mask that represented darker aspects of himself. As he began to explore his connection to the mask, it soon became clear to him that it contained all that he despised and considered to be not likable about himself. By taking on these qualities into his body and identifying with them and exploring them further through a form of dance that Ms. Scott refers to as spirit dancing, he was able to reconnect with the disavowed meanings this mask held for him (see Photo 2.2).

At the conclusion of each performance of his dance, Craig was greeted by many members of the audience who congratulated him on his brilliant performance and commented that watching his dance had put them in touch with aspects of themselves that they had not dared to look at directly within themselves before.

RECEPTIVE CONSCIOUSNESS AND THE BRIDGING OF ORDINARY WITH EXTRAORDINARY REALITY THROUGH THE CREATION OF ILLUSORY EXPERIENCE AND OBJECTS

The creation of a receptive potential space is a critical component of the healing art-making process involved in the negotiation of difficult life transitions. Such a state makes it possible for us to find the proper emotional distance to unpleasant and fearful aspects of ourselves that ordinarily we dare not acknowledge or wish to address. The shift to a receptive state of consciousness allows us to become relaxed and to focus directly upon our sensory, bodily-felt, imaginal internal experience.

Schore (2001) has noted that at the beginning of the twentieth century, Freud (1912/1958) proposed that the therapist turn his unconscious, like a receptive organ, toward the transmitting unconscious of his patient in order to reconstruct the patient's own unconscious. He referred to the state of receptive readiness that psychoanalysts should assume as one of "evenly suspended attention."

In 1973, Ornstein found that, while awake, we function within an active state of consciousness in which the sympathetic nervous system and striate muscle activity, as well as object-based logic and goal-oriented consciousness, prevail. By shifting to a more receptive, relaxed state of consciousness, our attention is drawn inward toward our internal subjective experience, which encompasses sensations, bodily-felt reactions, fantasies, and intuitions. While in a receptive state of consciousness, our parasympathetic nervous system and sensory-perceptual activities assume dominance. In this receptive state, our perceptual scope widens and our attention becomes more evenly divided. All of these physical characteristics enable us to bypass the automatic censor and defensive responses that generally accompany our more active state of consciousness; which is characterized by a narrower perceptual field and a more focused type of attention (Ornstein, 1973).

A review of current neurobiological studies conducted by Schore (2001) reveals greater right hemispheric brain involvement than left hemispheric involvement in the unconscious processing of affect-evoking stimuli. For instance, a neuroimaging study performed by Morris, Ohman, and Dolan (1998) showed that the unsconscious processing of emotional stimuli was specifically associated with the activation of the right hemisphere of the brain. Addressing the neurological level of interpersonal interactions that take place within a psychotherapeutic environment, Schore posits that

nonverbal transference-countertransference interactions that take place at preconscious-unconscious levels represent right hemisphere to right hemisphere communications of fast-acting, automatic, regulated and dysregulated emotional states between patient and therapist (p. 315).

Within the potential space created by creative arts therapists, various arts media can be used as instruments of consciousness to mediate and bridge ordinary, conscious reality with less conscious, extraordinary reality. By shifting from an active state of consciousness to a receptive state of consciousness, we can begin to make direct contact with less rational, less consciously enacted, imaginal and metaphoric realms of self-experience (Dosamantes-Alperson, 1979). Our capacity to bridge active with receptive states of consciousness relies upon our ability to move with ease between left-brain and right-brain states and upon our capacity to organize and derive the symbolic meaning contained in our illusory experience and creations.

The metaphors that we spontaneously generate from our illusory self-experience allow us to reframe the way we think about the world. This is possible because metaphors allow us to denote one kind of object or idea by drawing an analogy to another object or idea that bears a subjective semblance to it (Beth, 1977; Moore & Yamamoto, 1988). The meaning of a familiar, commonplace object or idea can become transformed into a novel object or idea by virtue of its being embedded within a new context. Creative arts therapists encourage their clients to transform their illusory subjective self-experience into spontaneously generated, enacted movements, sounds, rhythms, visual objects, dramatic enactments, and word metaphors in order to "see the same old thing in a fresh new way."

Within a creative arts therapies context, a therapist's capacity to perceive and to respond to her client's subjective experience requires that she be able to empathize with her client's experience (that is, to see the world through her client's eyes). This involves being able to perceive the client's less conscious communications by: (a) dropping down to a congruent state of consciousness that allows her to perceive her client's self-experience in a receptive, bodily-felt way, (b) locating the client's creative illusory self-experiences within the developmental-relational context of the client's intra- and interpersonal relationships, and (c) finding some way to communicate this understanding to the client in a language that the client can comprehend.

Chapter 3 addresses the developmental foundations of the developmental-relational arts-based model proposed in this book.

REFERENCES

American Psychiatric Association. (1994). *Diagnostic and statistical manual of mental disorders* (4th ed.). Washington, DC.

Barnes, M., & Berke, J. (1991). *Mary Barnes: Two approaches of a journey through madness.* London: Free Association Books.

Beth, M. (1977). *The process of thinking.* New York: David McKay.

Bettelheim, B. (1989). *The uses of enchantment: The meaning and importance of fairy tales.* New York: Vintage Books, Random House.

Campbell, J. (1956). *The hero with a thousand faces.* New York: The World Publishing Company.

Dosamantes-Alperson, E. (1979). The intrapsychic and the interpersonal in experiential movement psychotherapy. *American Journal of Dance Therapy, 3,* 20–31.

Dosamantes-Beaudry, I. (1998). Regression-reintegration. Central psycho-dynamic principle in rituals of transition. *Arts in Psychotherapy Journal, 25* (2), 79–84.

Eliade, M. (1995). *Rites and symbols of initiation: The mysteries of birth and rebirth* (2nd ed.). Woodstock, CT: Norton.

Erikson, E. H. (1968). *Identity, youth and crisis.* New York: Norton.

Freud, S. (1958). Recommendations to physicians practising psychoanalysis. In *The standard edition of the complete psychological works of Sigmund Freud* (Vol. 12, pp. 147–156). London: Hogarth Press. (Original work published 1912)

Gibbs, N. (2001, November 19). We gather together. *Time,* pp. 29–41.

Halifax, J. (1982). *Shaman: The wounded healer.* New York: Crossroad.

Janus, L. (1990). Fantasies of regression to the womb and rebirth as central elements of the psychotherapeutic process. *Journal of Prenatal and Perinatal Studies,* 89–100.

Jung, C. G. (1968). *Analytical psychology: Its theory and practice.* New York: Vintage Books.

Katz, E. (1982). *Boiling energy.* Cambridge, MA: Harvard University Press.

Keen, S. (1991). The enemy-maker. In C. Zweig & J. Abrams (Eds.), *Meeting the shadow: The hidden power of the dark side of human nature* (pp. 197–202). Los Angeles: Jeremy P. Tarcher.

Klinkenborg, V. (2001, October 30). Cultural predictions in the wake of the terrorist attack. *The New York Times, Editorials/Letters,* p. 12.

Knafo, D. (2002). Revising Ernst Kris's concept of regression in the service of the ego in art. *Psychoanalytic Psychology, 19* (1), 24–29.

Koestler, A. (1977). In W. Anderson (Ed.), *Therapy and the arts* (pp. 3–10). New York: Harper & Row.

Kris, E. (1952). *Psychoanalytic explorations in art.* New York: International Universities Press.

Kubie, L. (1961) *Neurotic distortion of the creative process.* New York: Noonday Press.

Laing, R. D. (1967). *The politics of experience.* New York: Ballantine Books.

Laing, R. D. (1969). *The politics of the family and other essays.* New York: Random House.

Mahler, M. S., Pine, F., & Bergman, A. (1975). *The psychological birth of the human infant: Symbiosis and individuation.* New York: Basic Books.

Meade, M. (1995). Introduction. In E. Eliade (Ed.), *Rites and symbols of initiation* (2nd ed., pp. ix–xxiv). Woodstock, CT: Spring Publications.

Moore, C., & Yamamoto, K. (1988). *Beyond words.* New York: Gordon and Breach Science.

Morris, J. S., Ohman, A., & Dolan, R. J. (1998). Conscious and unconscious emotional learning in the human amygdala. *Nature, 393,* 467–470.

Myers, J. E. (1988). The mid/late life generation gap. Adult children with aging parents. *Journal of Counseling and Development, 66,* 331–335.

Ogden, T. H. (1986). On projective identification. *International Journal of Psychoanalysis, 60,* 357–373.

Ornstein, R. E. (1973). *The psychology of consciousness.* New York: Viking Press.

Price, R. H., & Denner, B. (1973). *The making of a mental patient.* New York: Holt, Rinehart and Winston.

Sandler, J., & Sandler, A. M. (1994). Theoretical and technical comments on regression and anti-regression. *International Journal of Psycho-Analysis, 75,* 431–439.

Schoop, T., & Mitchell, P. (1974). *Won't you join the dance?* Palo Alto, CA: National Press Books.

Schore, A. N. (2001). Minds in the making: Attachment, the self-organizing brain, and developmentally-oriented psychoanalytic psychotherapy. *British Journal of Psychotherapy, 17* (3), 299–328.

Schuster, C. A., & Ashburn, S. S. (1992). *The process of human development: A holistic life-span approach* (3rd ed.). Philadelphia, PA: J. B. Lippincott.

Stewart, I. J. (2000). *Sacred woman sacred dance.* Rochester, VT: Inner Traditions International.

Szasz, T. S. (1973). *The age of madness.* Garden City, NY: Anchor Books.

Terr, L. (1990). *Too scared to cry.* New York: Harper Collins.

Turner, V. (1987). Betwixt and between: The limenal period of rites of passage. In L. Carus Madhi, S. Foster, & M. Little (Eds.), *Betwixt and between: Patterns of masculine and feminine initiation* (pp. 3–19). LaSalle, IL: Open Court.

Van Gennep, A. (1960). *The rites of passage.* Chicago: University of Chicago Press.

Winnicott, D. W. (1982). *Playing and reality.* New York: Penguin Books.

Zweig, C., & Abrams, J. (1991). *Meeting the shadow: The hidden power of the dark side of human nature.* Los Angeles: Jeremy P. Tarcher.

Zweig, C., & Wolff, S. (1997). *Romancing the shadow: Illuminating the dark side of the soul.* New York: Ballantine Books.

CHAPTER 3

The Intimate Social Sphere and the Origins of Potential Space, Illusory Experience, Creativity, and Self-Generativity

CONTEMPORARY PSYCHOSOCIAL STRESSORS AND RESILIENCE

During contemporary times, those of us who lead fast-paced Western modernist lifestyles find ourselves living longer lives, surrounded by a greater abundance of material comforts than previous generations have ever known before. However, simultaneously we are being challenged to respond to an ever-increasing number of psychosocial challenges that we experience as stressful (e.g., poverty, child neglect, youth violence, teen pregnancies, drug abuse, unemployment, homelessness, terrorism, and wars), all of which increase our vulnerability to serious illness.

Whenever a cataclysmic event happens without warning, it carries different meanings for each of us. Factors such as our physical proximity to the event, the seriousness of the losses that we have suffered, and our early experiences with loss, trauma, and family help to determine how well we will respond and adapt to the changes that we have experienced and how quickly we will recover from the tragedy. Although not all of us who witnessed the events of September 11, 2001, will be diagnosed with posttraumatic stress disorders, the lives of all who lived in this country through this period of history will be inexorably altered by the events that we have witnessed. Americans now live in a more uncertain, unpredictable world, where terrorism may strike in familiar surroundings at unexpected times. In order to understand our reactions to such intense, sudden, life-threatening changes, we need to understand how our sense of stability is derived, disrupted, and restored.

Our sense of self, self-worth, and trust in others is mediated within two kinds of psychosocial relationships: *intimate* and *public* (Taylor, 1994). The intimate social sphere is created with those who care for us early in life. In this sphere, we learn to emulate and to identify with those we care about and struggle against when they give us a hard time. Within the intimate sphere, we develop positive as well as negative kinds of identifications with those who matter to us in our lives. Later, as we begin to move away from our family of origin and enter school, the public social sphere is where we learn the social roles that our society expects us to fulfill. As we mature, we learn to negotiate the multiple collective identities that we create within the various social groups to which we belong. These groups are likely to differ with respect to such salient social features as age, gender, race, ethnicity, economic class, religion, and lifestyle.

INTIMATE SOCIAL SPHERE: CRUCIBLE FOR THE ACQUISITION OF SOCIAL SKILLS

Goleman (1995) has described the Western family as a "crucible," where children learn the skills they need to function effectively in their society (p. 189). This is an apt description because, in this country, it is still primarily within the context of the nuclear family that children receive continual input from their caregivers about who they are, their self-worth, and the quality of care and safety that is provided by the world in which they live.

Unfortunately, today many American families might more aptly be described as "cracked crucibles," because at present over nine million American children face multiple adverse family conditions that inhibit their ability to become productive and functional members of their society (Casey Foundation, 1999). One in seven children in the United States live with families confronting at least four or more psychosocial stressors that negatively impact their future chances for success (e.g., living in a single-parent household, with a parent who lacks a high school education, is unemployed, and is emotionally uninvolved with them). Wallerstein and Blakeslee (1989) have reported that in the United States, one in every two marriages end in divorce, and the rates are even higher for second marriages. By the time children reach the age of 18 years, many will have experienced up to three divorces in their families.

Because the kind of family and community a person comes from seem to predict his or her susceptibility to stress when exposed to unanticipated catastrophic events, individuals from cultures that provide family stability, environmental safety, community support, and low drug rates are less likely to suffer from posttraumatic stress reactions than are those from families that do not provide these conditions (Fairbank, Schlenger, Saigh, & Davidson, 1995).

During times of crisis, our need for security and comfort appears to rise steeply and we tend to reach out to close loved ones for the satisfaction of these needs. Following the catastrophic events of September 11, 2001, many Americans reported the need to reprioritize their life objectives and many elected to make their families their top priority (Gibbs, 2001). Times of crisis seem to be particularly difficult for unattached people as well as children. In today's world, children fear dying in plane crashes and nuclear explosions, but most of all they fear losing their parents.

Empirical research conducted on the relationship between the chronic experience of certain emotions and the subsequent outbreak of serious illnesses reveals that repeated bouts of anger and anxiety cause chronic stress, which, in turn, compromises a person's immune function to the point of speeding the metastasis of cancer (Goleman, 1995). The experience of long-term, chronic stress also doubles a person's vulnerability to asthma, headaches, peptic ulcers, and heart disease, and hastens the onset of type 1 diabetes, susceptibility to viral infections, and plaque formation, which contributes to the onset of myocardial infarctions. Furthermore, the experience of chronic depression tends to make us more vulnerable to becoming ill and, once ill, to impede our chances for a medical recovery.

Personal Characteristics of Resilient Individuals

Despite these dire findings, there are many children and adults who, when exposed to the psychosocial conditions that cause chronic stress, somehow manage to transcend the negative impact of these stressful conditions. A key to their resilience can be found in some personal characteristics that they share. As a group, they seem able: (a) to learn from their mistakes and find it possible to convert tragedy into challenge, (b) to achieve a sense of mastery over those aspects of their lives that matter and interest them, which, in turn, provides them with a sense of self-worth and confidence, (c) to treat themselves and others with respect, and (d) to turn to at least one charismatic adult for emotional support and guidance during times of need or trouble (Brooks & Goldstein, 2001; Csikszentmihalyi, 1990; Goleman, 1995).

These findings suggest that, if we want to lessen our levels of stress and lead more gratifying lives, we not only have to lessen the number and rate of psychosocial stressors we confront in our daily lives, but because this is not always possible, it is more important that we acquire the emotional and cognitive skills will that help us become more resilient to the psychosocial stressors that we do encounter. Simply acquiring great material wealth does not seem to guarantee our ability to cope well with stress nor to improve the quality of the lives that we lead (Csikszentmihalyi, 1990: Goleman, 1995).

HUMAN ATTACHMENT AND THE DEVELOPMENT
OF TRUST AND AFFECTIVE ATTUNEMENT

Rosenberg and Trevathan (2001) report that our human need for physical and emotional support seems to have evolutionary roots within the human birthing process itself. These anthropologists contend that the challenge of big-brained infants, a human pelvis designed for walking upright, and a rotational delivery in which the baby emerges facing backward have favored the evolution of assistance-seeking behavior during the birthing process in order to compensate for these difficulties. This may explain why attended births are a near universal feature of human cultures.

Even among the !Kung of southern Africa's Kalahari Desert—who are well known for viewing solitary birth as a cultural ideal—women do not usually manage to give birth alone until they have delivered several babies, at which mothers, sisters and other women are present (p. 75).

The critical importance of being able to turn to at least one competent and idealized adult to whom we can look up to and rely upon for support during times of crisis cannot be underestimated. This need is particularly great when we become the victims of sudden and unexpected acts of violence because, when this occurs, we experience ourselves as having been intentionally targeted for acts of malevolence, which shatters our assumptions about the constancy of the world, the trustworthiness of people, and the interpersonal world in general. In an instant, the social world becomes transformed into a dangerous place to be and people become potential threats to our safety (Goleman, 1995).

This fear was disconfirmed on September 11, 2001, when many brave firemen, police officers, and doctors rushed into the disintegrating Twin Towers of the World Trade Center to save the lives of strangers at the risk of losing theirs. Because of their courageous actions, these service-oriented people became the objects of mass adulation; they helped to restore Americans' faith and trust in humanity (Harden, 2001). On the same day, other acts of altruism and compassion from ordinary people were reported by the news media, which reminded us of our potential for compassion toward others, such as when the occupants of the Twin Towers carried disabled strangers from the burning buildings to safety, or when one friend made the choice to die because he refused to leave his disabled best friend behind to die alone. These examples of service and sacrifice inspired and touched us deeply because, during times of crisis, our need for altruism and compassion rises steeply, which helps to explain why, during 2002, children's preferred choice of Halloween costumes shifted from the monsters of previous years to public service people, such as firemen, policemen, and nurses.

In reviewing the personal histories of youth who had committed heinous acts of violence at their schools, Sullivan (2001) found two psychosocial precursors that all perpetrators shared in common: social isolation
and the absence of a "charismatic adult" to whom these youth might have
been able to turn to for mentorship, counsel, and support (p. 35). Unfortunately, as a nation we have largely ignored our youth's need for stable,
caring, mentoring relationships in which the relational and affective skills
they need to cope with difficult life transitions are learned and practiced.
One explanation for why this is the case is that within our patriarchal
society, the realm of social relationships and the expression of emotions
has tended to be seen as primarily the domain of women and therefore
associated with softness and not deserving of social recognition and value.
Miller (1976) and Gilligan (1982) have noted that in the United States
women have been socially penalized for showing concern for the welfare
of others and for their capacity to maintain emotional relatedness with
others.

Women not only define themselves in a context of human relationships but also
judge themselves in terms of their ability to care. Women's place in man's life cycle
has been that of nurturer, caretaker and helpmate, the weaver of those networks
of relationships on which she in turn relies. But while women have thus taken
care of men, men have, in their theories of psychological development, as in their
economic arrangements, tended to assume or devalue that care. When the focus
on individuation and individual achievement extends into adulthood and maturity is equated with personal autonomy, concern with relationships appears as a
weakness of women rather than as a human strength (Gilligan, 1982, p. 17).

Miller (1976) cites the separation-individuation model of self-development
favored by many Western mental health care professionals as one expression of the way Western social scientists have tended to support and favor
phallocentric ideas. This theory equates the achievement of emotional
maturity with the achievement of autonomy and independence rather
than with the achievement of mutuality and interdependence with others
(Mahler, Pine, & Bergman, 1975). Miller (1976) contends that at birth an
interactive sense of self is present among infants of both sexes but that girls
are soon socialized to become attentive to the needs of others and are con-
ditioned to get along with others, whereas boys are more frequently re-
warded for taking individual, independent action against and over others.
   Morgan (2001) claims that historically, cross-culturally, and internationally, well over 80 percent of militant insurgents or "terrorists" have been
males between the ages of 22 and 25 years who have conceived their acts
of violence as an integral part of "manhood struggles." However, because
of their rarity, female terrorists have received disproportionate attention
from the media. According to Morgan, women who become involved with

terrorist causes tend to do so because of their attachment to a male who is heavily involved with terrorist activities. This author uses the term "demon-lover syndrome" to refer to this form of attachment.

For women, the dark side of being raised in a patriarchal society, is that they, too, have internalized the sexist values of their society. Chessler (2001) has pointed out that one drawback of learning to placate and to please others is that women learn to interpret the criticism they receive from others in terms of disconnection and abandonment. This makes it difficult for them to express their aggression directly. Instead, many find indirect ways to express their aggression, such as through gossip, slander, and ostracism aimed primarily at their own gender.

Attachment Theory

Our need for an idealized adult whom we can admire and identify with early in life and to whom we can subsequently turn to for support and guidance originally manifests itself within the context of the first emotional relationship that we forge with one or several adults of either sex who are charged with our care.

Attachment theory is a developmental theory that focuses on the role that primary caregivers serve as a secure base from which infants may explore and learn about their environment. Attachment theory also focuses upon the first relationship as the context for socialization and the development of expectations about close relationships (Posada & Jacobs, 2001). The term "attachment" refers to the emotional bond that infants develop with one or a few selected persons by the age of seven months (Bowlby, 1973). Attachment can be observed in the intense concern for the whereabouts of the primary caregiver that young children show when they are in unfamiliar surroundings. During early childhood and later in more subtle, less explicit forms, attachment can be observed by the insistent interest a person shows in maintaining close proximity to the bonded person. The bonded person appears to serve as a source of emotional security as well as a secure base for the exploration of unfamiliar environments.

In our society, the primary responsibility for the care of infants still falls primarily upon the mother. The attachments we form with our mothers can be emotionally secure or not. Infants whose first attachments are secure tend to perceive and to expect the world around them to be safe, secure, and predictable, whereas those who develop insecure attachments with their caregivers tend to grow up believing that the world around them is an inhospitable, unpredictable, and a threatening place to be. Ainsworth, Blehar, Waters, and Wall (1978) have identified three organized patterns of infant responses to separation from and reunion with their mothers: secure, ambivalent, and avoidant. More recently, Main (2000) has added a fourth attachment style, the disorganized type.

Infants are emotionally vulnerable to separations from their primary caregivers. Spitz (1945) studied institutionalized children who had been separated from their mothers at various ages and found that children who had been separated from their mothers between the ages of six months and one year were most susceptible to becoming anaclitically depressed (i.e., they exhibited cognitive and emotional delays, were unresponsive to outside stimulation, and became socially withdrawn). When children experience prolonged separations from their primary caregivers, they tend to react in an emotionally predictable pattern: they first protest their caregivers' departure, then they become despondent and depressed, and, finally, they become resigned and detached from others and their environment (Bowlby, 1973).

When children are given an opportunity to forge secure attachments with their mothers, they are able to tolerate brief separations from them, and then, when reunited with their mothers, they are able to resume contact with them. In contrast, children who are insecurely attached tend to either under- or overreact emotionally to their mother's departure, and then upon their mother's return, to resist physical contact with them (Ainsworth et al., 1978). Disorganized or disoriented behavior occurs whenever a child is frightened of his or her primary caregiver or other significant attachment figure. This disorganization may appear as a result of the child being directly maltreated or even as a "second-generation effect" resulting from the parents' own experiences with fright or trauma, which are subsequently passed on to their offspring, as is the case of some offspring whose parents have survived the Holocaust of World War II (Hesse & Maine, 1999).

THE FIRST INTERSUBJECTIVE RELATIONSHIP, THE ORIGINS OF POTENTIAL SPACE, AND THE CREATION OF ILLUSORY EXPERIENCE AND OBJECTS

In 1965, Winnicott proclaimed that "the inherited potential of an infant cannot become an infant unless linked to maternal care" (p. 43), by which he meant that an infant's sense of self evolves only within the context of an ongoing, interactive, intersubjectve relationship that is constructed by the child with a caregiver. Stolorow and Atwood (1992) have defined the term intersubjectivity as the mutual interplay that takes place between the subjective worlds of mother and infant or later within the context of a psychoanalytic relationship established between an analyst and an analysand. Josselson (2000) contends that intersubjectivity follows a developmental trajectory, in which increased knowledge of one's self is acquired in tandem with an increased knowledge of others.

According to Winnicott (1965), the "good enough mother" is one who not only "meets the omnipotence of the infant" but also "to some extent makes sense of it" (p. 145). In contrast, the mother who is "not good enough . . . is not able to implement the infant's omnipotence, and so she repeatedly fails to meet the infant's gesture; instead she substitutes her own gesture," demanding compliance from the infant to her demands (p. 145). Winnicott (1965) considered the initial caregiver's provision of "a good enough holding environment" to be essential to the infant's welfare. Through the provision of an affectively attuned and caring environment, a child comes to acquire the capacity for self-soothing during the mother's absence.

Once children have achieved the capacity to be comforted when alone, they proceed to achieve a critical developmental landmark, the creation of the first *transitional object*. A transitional object is an inanimate concrete object, such as a blanket or teddy bear, that bears a sensory and an emotional relationship to a toddler's own mother and comes to be appropriated and transformed by the toddler into an illusory object that holds magical meaning for her or him (Winnicott, 1982, p. 1). The creation of the first transitional object represents the child's first creative act.

Initially, children fill the intermediate or potential space created by their mother's departure with illusory images and objects, and then with creative solitary play involving these objects. According to Winnicott (1982) "there is a direct development from transitional phenomena to playing, and from playing to shared playing, and from this to cultural experiences" (p. 60). Our creation of the first transitional or illusory object, therefore, heralds our later capacity to play with objects, symbols, and metaphors in creative, regenerative ways. Children who have been seriously emotionally deprived as infants seem unable to create gratifying transitional objects. They "rigidly clutch to fetish-objects, without play, without enjoyment and without libido-investment" (Deri, 1978, p. 53).

Psychoanalysts use the term mirroring to refer to the mother's capacity to accurately perceive her child's inner states (Goleman, 1995). Stern (1985) has described in detail various senses of self (including the sense of agency, sense of self-coherence, sense of self-affectivity, and sense of going on being) that a child comes to acquire within the intersubjective relationship that is conjointly constructed by parent and child. He coined the term "affective attunement" to refer to how accurately our early emotional experience is perceived, accepted, and reciprocated by our caregivers (Stern, pp. 140–142). The cumulative impact of early affective attunements and misattunements appears to be instrumental in shaping the relational patterns and expectations that we subsequently bring to other intimate relationships as we mature.

Affectively attuned parents are able to resonate with their children's emotional states and can share and amplify their children's positive emotional states while reducing negative states. According to Siegel (1999), the attachment patterns that children establish with their caregivers directly shape their developing brain, particularly the orbitofrontal cortex area. The mutual sharing or co-constructing of narratives that children create in concert with their caregivers about lived events serves to elaborate their internal experiences further. Relationships that are connecting help to support the development of many domains, including social, emotional, and cognitive ones, whereas those that elicit uncomfortable emotional states in children or parents tend to result in a relational disconnection between them.

Johnson (1998) has pointed out that *tolerable* missattunements, discrepancies, and incompatibilities are also necessary, however, to stimulate the child's further development. This observation is supported by Piaget's (1972) findings that it is only during moments when children's experience is at odds with others' perceptions, that they experience cognitive dissonance, and therefore must actively search for ways to reorganize their view of the world so as to minimize the emotional discrepancy they experience as a result of being at odds with the consensual reality that is presented by others.

A "good enough mother" is not only someone who can affectively attune herself to her child's subjective experience, but also someone who can sense when to introduce a delay between the infant's needs and her gratification of those needs (Deri, 1978). By adequately gauging her infant's emotional states, the mother becomes a model for her child's own developing capacity for affective attunement and empathic behavior toward others. To be empathic toward others means that the child must be able "to identify with or vicariously experience the feelings, thoughts and attitudes of others" (Brooks & Goldstein, 2001, p. 17).

Gardner (1993) has distinguished two kinds of knowledge that help us differentiate our emotions and behave empathically toward others. He refers to these skills as "intrapersonal and interpersonal intelligences," respectively (pp. 22–25). Intrapersonal intelligence encompasses such internal aspects as having access to a range of emotions, as well as the capacity to differentiate and label our emotions, and to use our emotions to guide our behavior. Interpersonal intelligence refers to a person's ability to perceive the moods, temperaments, motivations, and intentions of others and to use this knowledge to understand other people. Both of these emotional intelligences evolve and develop with the context of the first significant relationships we forge with those adults who care for us.

Human Modes of Experience and Expression

A constructivist approach to human development assumes that humans possess a form-seeking and meaning-making part of themselves that motivates them to produce a narrative accounting of who they are, and why they do whatever they do (Gusman et al., 1996). Whenever catastrophic events occur, humans tend to cling to what they know and, as a result, they are liable to become rigid and perseverative in their responses to stress. When their behavior becomes inflexible, they find it difficult to draw new meanings. Effective therapists work to open the perceptual field of traumatized persons in order to restore their ability to become active and flexible interpreters of their own self-experience.

As humans we have access to three modes of perceiving, responding to, and symbolizing our subjective experience: enactive, imagistic, and lexical. Each of these modes of knowing offers us a unique view of the world and ourselves that is useful to our adjustment in the world. These modes become available to us at various developmental stages prior to the age of two years (Horowitz, 1970). The enactive mode is available to us from birth. This mode refers to action tendencies we express through our body movements, gestures, and postures. Much of the emotional meaning that we convey to others about ourselves when relating to them is conveyed through this mode (Dosamantes-Alperson, 1980; Rosenthal, Hall, Di Matteo, Rogers, & Archer, 1977). Rosenthal et al. (1977) have found that over 90 percent of the emotional meaning in human communications is carried on implicitly through enactive modes of expression (e.g., the volume, tone, and rhythm of our voices, gestures, postures, and body movements).

The imagistic mode refers to sensory experiences that are transmitted through visual, auditory, tactile, and proprioceptive senses. We acquire our capacity for visual imagery when we are able to mentally re-create a representation of an absent object, a developmental landmark that usually occurs between the sixth or seventh month of age (Piaget, 1972). One virtue of this mode of knowing is that a great deal of meaning can be carried and contained within a single image (Dosamantes-Alperson, 1981, 1985). For instance, dream images contain multiple meanings that are condensed and represented through a single image.

The third mode of knowing, the lexical mode, communicates meaning through word symbols. This mode is acquired at about the age of two years, when we begin to communicate symbolically to others through words. This mode offers us the freedom to detach from our direct sensory experience of objects in the environment. This feature has the advantage of allowing us to think and to communicate with others analytically and abstractly through consensually culturally shared symbols. However, this advantage can become a disadvantage, when we use this mode to distance ourselves from our own bodily-felt experience and emotions, and thereby reduce our capacity to perceive the world and ourselves somatically. This is a disadvantage because our capacity for somatic perception is what allows us to track the emotional tenor of whatever social situations we find ourselves in, including toxic relationships that may be harmful to us and can cause us to become seriously ill (Jourard, 1974; Lowen, 1970; Reich, 1949).

Among adults these three ways of knowing function in a seamless, integrated manner. However, because our society has tended to compartmentalize and to suppress the outward expression of nonverbal modes of knowing through its socialization and educational practices, these modes usually function automatically out of our conscious awareness (Dosamantes-Beaudry, 1997; Fisher, 1973; Lowen, 1970). Fisher has noted:

Our culture is dedicated to blunting the individual's skills in interpreting body experiences. Most "advanced" cultures strive for rationality and regard body arousal as likely to mislead or to introduce irrationality into decision-making. The child is taught to make decisions "with his head." If he says that he does not "feel like" doing something, this is usually regarded as a pretty flimsy basis for acting. Action must be based on rational "reasons" rather than body feelings. Even basic body feelings like hunger or the need to defecate are typically relegated to the control of more cognitively oriented schedules, which dictate when it is proper to respond to such feelings (p. 11).

The Development of Various Kinds of Play

As children mature and begin to separate from their caregivers, playing becomes a major activity that they engage in voluntarily and spontaneously for pleasure (Schuster & Ashburn, 1992). Through play, children discover who they are and learn to master the various physical and social competencies they need to function in the world at their own pace and free from outside constraints. Human beings' capacity for play seems to follow a developmental trajectory. For example, between the ages of three and six years, children begin to engage in make-believe sociodramatic play with other children that allows them to try on many hats and to enact many of the social roles that they will later assume as adults. Through pretend play, children learn to develop the social skills that they need to interact successfully with their peers, to gain insight into adult roles, and to acquire a sense of responsibility and concern for the feelings of others (Smilansky, 1968). Pretend play is a way of preparing children for the novel and the unexpected (Azar, 2002).

Piaget (1972) defined play as pure assimilation. His definition emphasized the fact that playful behavior is repeated simply for the sheer pleasure of it. Psychoanalysts highlight the psychodynamic aspects of play and emphasize its wish-fulfilling aspects. They stress that make-believe play and fantasy make the pain of consensual reality more tolerable (Schuster & Ashburn, 1992). Children who are able to engage in make-believe play and wish-fulfilling fantasies seem to be afforded some degree of immunity against the deleterious effects produced by catastrophic events (Terr, 1990). Commenting upon the ways in which the children of New York City coped with the catastrophic events of September 11, 2001, child psychoanalyst Elsa First (2002) observed:

Looking at the ways of coping and metabolizing trauma, I was impressed by how profoundly impelled children were to create symbolic representations—especially of the burning and collapsing towers—in drawings, painting, play and narrative. A rift in reality had to be repaired (p. 44).

Hurlock (1978) has described the developmental stages that Western children's play behavior tends to follow:

1. *Exploratory state.* During the first year of life, children explore their own bodies and their environment through their bodies, body movement, and sensory experience.
2. *Toy state.* From the age of one year to toddlerhood, children begin to engage in make-believe or pretend play and to collect toys that initially they do not want to share with other children. (Smilansky [1968] claims that symbolic play begins at about two years of age when children begin to combine reality with magic to fulfill their wishful fantasies and emotional needs. Then, at about four years of age, toddlers become engaged in make-believe play. They pretend to be someone else by imitating others' speech and actions.)
3. *Play stage.* School-aged children continue to play with toys but gradually begin to develop games that have structure and are determined by social rules (e.g., they engage in sports activities that involve their peers and require skills that are regulated by a preestablished set of rules).
4. *Daydreaming stage.* During latency at about seven years of age, children acquire the capacity to daydream, which involves the internalization of wish-fulfilling fantasies and replaces the concrete make-believe play of earlier years. At this age, reading becomes a favorite pastime of Western children.

Our need to create illusory, creative experiences does not end in latency but continues throughout our lives. The creation of illusory experience is what colors our lives with a sense of awe, mastery, and meaning (Kubie, 1961; Langer, 1953). Our capacity to create illusory experience seems to follow a developmental trajectory that increasingly assumes more complex symbolic forms, engages others, and becomes interiorized (e.g., as evidenced by the daydreams and night dreams that adults produce). In adulthood, we are able to reconnect with earlier forms of illusion making through the process of regression. (The central role played by regression in the process of self-reintegration was discussed in chapter 2.)

POTENTIAL SPACE, CREATIVITY, AND SELF-GENERATIVITY

Based on process research that he conducted with adult clients engaged in client-centered therapy, Rogers (1962) concluded that the same process that facilitates creative activities across various fields of human endeavor, from the arts through the sciences, also facilitates the self-transformative process that occurs during successful client-centered therapy. He defined the creative process as "the emergence of a novel relational product, growing out of the uniqueness of the individual on the one hand, and the material, events, people or circumstances in his life on the other" (p. 65).

Rogers (1962) considered creativity to be a process that offers people an opportunity for self-generativity, provided certain external and internal conditions were met. He discovered that when clients were accepted unconditionally, were understood empathically, and were granted the freedom to express themselves symbolically without the fear of being judged, they began to change in the direction of becoming more open to their experience, more trusting of their experience as a guide for their behavior, and more willing to play spontaneously with ideas, things, and relationships.

Creative arts therapists are therapists who are trained to directly facilitate their clients' creative potential for self-generativity. Although they are experts in the therapeutic use of a particular art medium, they all share in common an arts-based-process approach to healing that encompasses the following steps: (a) they facilitate the conditions that help to promote the emergence of a creative "potential space"; (b) in this space, they encourage clients to regress and to become immersed in the creation of illusion making, in pretend playing, and in the novel manipulation of objects, symbols, and metaphors that they derive from their own experience and imagination; (c) they help clients work through the various meanings contained in their symbolic and expressive behavior.

Within the context of a relaxed, receptive environment facilitated by a creative arts therapist, it becomes possible for adults to regress and to become actively engaged in the creative art-making process outlined earlier. Johnson (1998) refers to the potential space facilitated by creative arts therapists as an "arts/playspace" (p. 91). As an aspect of their training, creative arts therapists learn how to modify their methods to meet their clients at the emotional developmental level at which they happen to be in the moment.

Second Chances

During the course of progressing through the life cycle, Western children gradually learn to expand and to transfer their love of self to their mothers, then to other family members, then to peers, and finally to other significant adults. The emotional derailments that occur as a result of early misattunements are often revisited by them during later stages of development (Stern, 1985; Stolorow & Atwood, 1992). Growing up gives human beings a second chance to find better coping strategies and more satisfying solutions for transitions that remain unresolved for them.

Sometimes they are also fortunate enough to have a caring, charismatic adult around them who is willing to act as a mentor to them and who can point out more effective ways of resolving the challenges that they encounter. When people become overwhelmed by circumstances that are beyond their capacity to handle, they may turn to healers, including creative arts therapists, to help them restore their emotional balance, find new meaning, and recover their sense of relatedness to others.

What propels people to seek a healing or therapeutic relationship is usually the experience of intense psychological pain or their repetition of relational patterns that no longer seem appropriate to the situation or emotionally fulfilling to them (Freud, 1914/1958). Johnson (1998) maintains that within the "arts/playspace" created within a creative arts therapies context, clients are able to connect to inner states that can be projected not only onto their therapist, but also onto the safer art medium, where they can be worked through and become assimilated by the client into a more benign form (p. 86).

HUMAN NEED FOR A MENTORING RELATIONSHIP WITH A CHARISMATIC ADULT

During times of crisis, our need for an idealized other to whom we can turn to for support and guidance is heightened. The person to whom we turn must not only be someone who shares our worldview, but also someone who possesses a particular set of idealized personal characteristics that we associate with a wise person.

Psychoanalysts use the term transference to refer to emotionally positive and negative reactions that analysands project onto their analyst. Freud (1914/1958, 1915/1958) viewed these reactions as repetitions of past relationships that had been established early in life with significant others. These reactions are particularly valuable in allowing analysts to reconstruct their analysands' past relationships. Transference reactions also provide analysands with an opportunity to gain access to those relationships that they have not been able to assimilate into their current life experience.

During times of crisis, all of us require a relationship with an empathic person who can serve to shore up our faltering sense of self. Kohut (1980) coined the term "selfobject" to refer to the fact that many of his analysands used him as a functional part of themselves. This was particularly the case with those persons who experienced difficulties in maintaining a cohesive sense of self. Kohut (1977) also maintained that all of us throughout our lives have a need to idealize persons whom we admire and from whom we would like to receive acknowledgment.

Because creative arts therapists serve in the role of mediators between material and imaginal realms, their clients frequently expect them to exhibit those personal qualities that Young-Eisendrath and Miller (2000) found to be associated with "mature spirituality," namely, integrity, wisdom, and a capacity for transcendence. This means that, ideally, creative arts therapists are persons who are able to synthesize multiple layers of meaning, tolerate ambiguous or paradoxical situations, demonstrate a high level of insightfulness, and readily connect phenomenal reality to symbols. They also need to be able to contain the unpleasant feelings that their clients' negative projections generate within them, understand the relational meanings contained in their clients' spontaneously enacted symbolic behavior and experiential metaphors, and not be afraid to deviate from the therapeutic frame in which they have been trained.

Some personal characteristics that clients have described as being associated with therapists' effectiveness include (a) self-insight which refers to the extent to which therapists are aware of their own feelings and understand the basis for them; (b) empathic ability, which consists of a partial or trial identification by therapists with their clients' emotional experience while not losing themselves in the process; (c) self-integration which includes the capacity for self-differentiation and the ability to put aside their personal needs in favor of their clients' needs; (d) anxiety management skills, which determine how well therapists manage their anxiety in the presence of clients' strong emotions; and (e) conceptualization ability, which refers to how well therapists think about clients' dynamics within the therapeutic relationship and within the context of their clients' past relationships (Van Wagoner, Gelso, Hayes, & Diemer, 1991).

Of course, all of these personal attributes and competencies represent a composite of the Western ideal of a wise person or charismatic other, which many of us who have been reared in these societies would like to see manifested in the persons to whom we turn to for guidance and emotional support during times of crisis. However, these are clearly idealized attributes and competencies that reflect our wish for the perfect parent. When we project such wishes onto a trained and well-intentioned but mortal and fallible person, we are inevitably bound to be disappointed. We can view the therapeutic relationship itself as a temporary illusory relationship that comes to an end when the client is finally able to perceive and to accept both himself and the therapist as mere mortal, fallible, ordinary human beings.

For clients, the emergence of such disappointment offers an opportunity to confront shadow aspects of themselves, that is, to discover the origins of their negative projections, to process the meaning contained in these projections, and to assimilate the meanings contained in these projections into their current life experience and relationships. The capacity to reclaim our projections by discovering the meaning that they hold for us is one critical feature that heralds the third and final phase of all healing transitions.

THE EMERGENCE OF THE CREATIVE ARTS THERAPIES FIELD: A CONTEMPORARY USE OF THE ARTS FOR HEALING

Each person has the potential to access what Estes (1995) refers to as the "Rio Abajo Rio," or the river beneath the river (or deep unconscious experience). This psychological space can be reached through various means such as "through deep meditation, dance, writing, painting, prayermaking, singing, drumming, active imagination, or any activity which requires an intense altered consciousness" (Estes, p. 30).

The integral role played by the arts in the healing rituals practiced by the shaman of traditional cultures has been well documented by anthropologists (Campbell, 1983; Halifax, 1982). Visions, dreams, and trances are central to the practice of shamanism. The shaman acts as a mediator between the spirit world and ordinary reality. Historically, as pre-Christian traditions were eradicated in western Europe, so too were the integrative functions played by the arts in the healing practices developed by early pre-Christian societies (Dosamantes-Beaudry, 2001; Redmond, 1997). As the arts became dissociated from the embodied experience of people's everyday life and from folk medicine, artists were relegated to the role of artisans for hire by religious and aristocratic patrons.

In the twentieth century, during the transitional period of the 1960s in this country, the healing practices that had been a part of pre-Christian traditions, however, began to resurface and to be rediscovered anew, largely because of the receptive and auspicious social conditions that were created by the humanistic psychology movement of the time. This movement was critical of mainstream Western culture's obsession with emotional control and rational thought. By exalting the value of embodied experience and by supporting the wide range of somatic healing practices, this movement sought to redress this cultural imbalance.

During the 1980s this movement, in turn, gave rise to the development of a subjective, individualistic form of spirituality that came to be known in this country as the New Age movement. Dissatisfied with mainstream culture's attachment to materialism and consumerism, but finding little meaning in Western organized religions, many persons who identified with this movement searched for ways to reconnect more personally to their own individual visions of sacredness. This movement provided a social platform for the expression and gratification of these individuals' spiritual needs.

Some of the women who identified with this movement later came to rediscover the history of matriarchal Goddess religions of antiquity and began to develop spiritual and healing practices that were inspired by and fashioned after these early religions. Walker (1990) claims that the religious rituals established by women who were searching for a spiritual connection set a lighter, more relational and democratic tone than that set by male religions, which placed undue emphasis on self-denial, self-abasement, suffering, and guilt. She states:

After centuries of suppression, the feminine spirit rises again to assert that divinity is discoverable through the senses; that laughter is not hostile to spirituality; that play can have profound resonances in human psychology and that members of a spiritually oriented group need not lead or be led, win or lose, but may cooperate in the creation of a group feeling to which each participant may relate in her own way (Walker, p. 22).

Within this historical-cultural context as a backdrop, arts practitioners interested in the use of the arts for healing, who had been working in relative isolation and obscurity in various regions of this country during the 1960s, came together to form national professional organizations that came to represent the educational and political interests of their respective arts therapies fields. A decade later, as these organizations grew in size, they began to reach out to one another. The alliances they formed helped them to forge a larger political umbrella for the collective and to stimulate cross-disciplinary contacts and dialogues among creative arts therapists. When the *Arts in Psychotherapy Journal,* a professional international journal, became a reality, it began to feature the written work of *all* creative arts therapists as well as scholars and clinicians from other disciplines who were interested in the use of various art forms as vehicles for transformation and healing.

At present most creative arts therapists are trained as interdisciplinary practitioners who follow the educational standards set by their respective professional associations. They are trained in the practice of at least one art therapy form and they also acquire a general knowledge of existing psychotherapeutic theories and methods. Their practices, therefore, reflect a synthesis of artistic and psychotherapeutic kinds of knowledge. To a greater or lesser degree, creative arts therapists also incorporate into their practices some of the more individualist spiritual elements that were introduced by the New Age movement.

As a group, creative arts therapists are experts in the facilitation of a healing art-making process that makes possible self- and communal transformation. For someone wishing to be trained in this field, the question of which creative arts therapy field to specialize in is likely to be determined by the primary art medium he or she feels most connected to and envisions using as a practitioner. Thus, art therapists are experts in the use of visual media. In their practices, art therapists make use of a variety of visual media to explore the meaning contained in the imagistic meta-phors and visual symbols their clients create (McNiff, 1997). Dance therapists are experts in the symbolic meaning enacted by clients through spontaneous therapeutic individual or group movement experiences. They make use of receptive and expressive forms of movement to promote their clients' physical and emotional integration and interpersonal sensitivity (Dosamantes-Beaudry, 1997). Music therapists are experts in the therapeutic use of rhythm and sound. They make use of receptive and expressive aspects of music to promote their clients' well-being and relatedness with others (Bonny, 1997). Drama therapists are experts in the use of dramatic enactment. They empower their clients through the use of role-playing techniques that help them integrate polarized aspects of their self-experience (Landy, 1997b). Poetry therapists are experts in the metaphoric use of language as a means of revealing and acknowledging less conscious aspects of their clients' self-experience (Lerner, 1997). In the near future, academic departments are likely to be created that will house all of the arts therapies encompassed by the creative arts therapies field within the same department (see the recommendations offered by the author in chapter 7).

The receptive and expressive art-making process facilitated by creative arts therapies through different arts media involves clients' temporary regression into the less conscious realm of pretend play and their return to the world of ordinary reality. The art-making process is an experiential process that can be thought of as a journey and a search for personal and collective meaning. This process facilitates clients' direct contact with less conscious aspects of their illusory self-experience. The symbols and metaphors that clients directly interact with through pretend play enable them to transform how they perceive themselves and others.

Commenting upon the unique contribution that the creative arts therapies can make within the psychotherapeutic arena, psychiatrist, Israel Zwerling (1989) observed:

The creative arts therapies evoke responses, precisely at the level at which psychotherapists seem to engage patients, more directly and more immediately than do any of the more traditional verbal therapies. The feelings that are aroused and expressed while singing or playing an instrument, or listening to music, or moving to a rhythm, or drawing or painting, become available to the therapist, to identify, to develop, and to change (p. 23).

Initially, creative arts therapists found employment within psychiatric mental health institutions as well as in private practice. In recent years, they have also begun to find work opportunities within educational, health, and welfare facilities concerned with illness prevention and community healing (Dosamantes-Beaudry, 1997). For instance, under the auspices of national and international welfare agencies that provide crisis intervention programs, some creative arts therapists have started to provide their services at sites where violent catastrophic events have erupted (Kalmanowitz & Lloyd, 1999; Lahad, 1999).

Healing Intentions of Creative Arts Therapies

In 1997, Robert Landy, a past editor-in-chief of the *Arts in Psychotherapy Journal*, described the creative arts therapies field as a coherent field. He noted that, although practitioners in the field came from various distinctive arts therapies disciplines (e.g., art therapy, dance/movement therapy, drama therapy and psychodrama, music therapy, and poetry therapy), each requiring specialized training in the unique art medium used, all shared in common the art-making process as a healing modality (Landy, 1997a). I would add that the healing, transformative effects generated by the art-making process used by all creative arts therapies take place within the context of three kinds of object relationships:

1. The subjective relationship and identifications that clients establish with the objects that they create from their own imagination or experience while actively mediating a problematic situation in their lives, as well as the subsequent experiential metaphors that emerge, help to open up the clients' perceptual field, so that they can view their problems from a fresh perspective.

2. The intersubjective relationship that clients create in collaboration with their therapist provides clients with a model for psychological functions they need to function more effectively within the outside world but do not possess at the outset of therapy.

3. The interpersonal relationship that clients establish with their therapist or members of their therapy group provides clients with feedback about their behavior as seen through the eyes of others and presents consensually validated norms of behavior against which clients can evaluate their own actions.

Within the contexts of everyday life and in the therapeutic environment, these relationships generally overlap and function in a seamless way relative to one another. However, because each type of object relationship makes a unique contribution to the promotion of self and communal change, the part played by each in making possible the successful mediation of difficult developmental and external transitions is highlighted in chapters 4 and 6.

Chapter 4 features the healing work of several creative arts therapists who have adopted an intimate developmental-relational approach to working with clients whose sense of self is tenuous or constricted as a result of having been exposed to the cumulative and deleterious effects of early developmental derailments. The case of a client who suddenly became structurally regressed as a result of being brutally raped and abducted is also presented.

REFERENCES

Ainsworth, M. D. S., Blehar, M. C., Waters, E., & Wall, S. (1978). *Patterns of attachment: Observations in the strange situation and at home.* Hillsdale, NJ: Erlbaum.

Azar, B. (2002, March). It's more than fun and games. *Monitor on Psychology, 33* (3), 50–51.

Bonny, H. L. (1997). The state of the art of music therapy. *Arts in Psychotherapy Journal, 24* (1), 65–73.

Bowlby, J. M. (1973). *Attachment and loss.* New York: Basic Books.

Brooks, R., & Goldstein, S. (2001). *Raising resilient children.* Lincolnwood, IL: Contemporary Publishing Group.

Campbell, J. (1983). *The way of the animal powers: Vol. 1.* London: Summerfield Press.

Casey Foundation. (1999). At greatest risk: Identifying America's most vulnerable children. In *Kids count data book.* Baltimore: Casey Foundation.

Chessler, P. (2001). *Woman's inhumanity to woman.* New York: Thunder's Mouth Press/Nation Books.

Csikszentmihalyi, M. (1990). *Flow: The psychology of optimal experience.* New York: Harper & Row.

Deri, S. (1978). Transitional phenomena: Vicissitudes of symbolization and creativity. In S. A. Grolnick, L. Barkin, & W. Muensterberger (Eds.), *Between reality and fantasy* (pp. 45–60). Northvale, NJ: Jason Aronson.

Dosamantes-Alperson, E. (1980). Contacting bodily-felt experiencing in psychotherapy. In J. E. Shorr, G. E. Sobel, P. Robin, & J. A. Connella (Eds.), *Imagery: Its many dimensions and applications* (pp. 223–241). New York: Plenum Press.

Dosamantes-Alperson, E. (1981). The interaction between movement and imagery in experiential movement psychotherapy. *Psychotherapy: Theory, Research and Practice, 18,* 266–270.

Dosamantes-Alperson, E. (1985). A current perspective of imagery in psychoanalysis. *Imagination, Cognition and Personality, 5* (3), 199–209.

Dosamantes-Beaudry, I. (1997). Reconfiguring identity. *Arts in Psychotherapy Journal, 24* (1), 51–57.

Dosamantes-Beaudry, I. (2001). The suppression and modern re-emergence of sacred feminine healing traditions. *Arts in Psychotherapy Journal, 28* (1), 31–37.

Estes, C. P. (1995). *Women who run with the wolves.* New York: Ballantine Books.

Fairbank, J. A., Schlenger, W. E., Saigh, P. A., & Davidson, J. R. T. (1995). An epidemiologic profile of post-traumatic stress disorder: Prevalence, co-morbidity, and risk factors. In M. A. Friedman, D. S. Charney, & A. V. Deutch (Eds.), *Neurobiological and clinical consequences of stress: From normal adaptation to post-traumatic stress disorder*. Philadelphia: Lippencott-Raven.

First, E. (2002). Opinion: The aftermath of September 11. Parents and children. *Newsletter of the International Psychoanalytic Association, 11* (1), 43–45.

Fisher, S. (1973). *Body consciousness*. Englewood Cliffs, NJ: Prentice Hall.

Freud, S. (1958). Remembering, repeating and working through (further recommendations on the technique of psychoanalysis). In *The standard edition of the complete works of Sigmund Freud* (Vol. 12, pp. 145–156). London: Hogarth Press. (Original work published 1914)

Freud, S. (1958). Observations on transference-love. In (Ed. and Trans.), *The standard edition of the complete works of Sigmund Freud* (Vol. 12, pp. 159–171). London: Hogarth Press. (Original work published 1915)

Gardner, H. (1993). *Multiple intelligences*. New York: Basic Books.

Gibbs, N. (2001, November 19). We gather together. *Time*, pp. 29–41.

Gilligan, C. (1982). *In a different voice*. Cambridge, MA: Harvard University Press.

Goleman, D. (1995). *Emotional intelligence*. New York: Bantam Books.

Gusman, F. D., Stewart, J., Hiley Young, B., Riney, S. J., Abueg, F. R., & Blake, D. D. (1996). A multicultural developmental approach to treating trauma. In A. J. Marsella, M. J. Friedman, E. T. Gerrity, & R. M. Scurfield (Eds.), *Ethnocultural aspects of posttraumatic stress disorders* (pp. 439–459). Washington, DC: American Psychological Association.

Halifax, J. (1982). *Shaman the wounded healer*. New York: Crossroad.

Harden, B. (2001, September 30). Flag fever: The paradox of patriotism. *The New York Times, Week in Review*, pp. 1, 5.

Hesse, E., & Main, M. (1999). Second-generation effects of unresolved trauma as observed in non-maltreating parents: Dissociated, frightened and threatening parental behavior. *Psychoanalytic Inquiry, 19*, 481–540.

Horowitz, M. J. (1970). *Image formation and cognition*. New York: Century Crofts.

Hurlock, E. B. (1978). *Child development* (6th ed.). New York: McGraw Hill.

Johnson, D. R. (1998). On the therapeutic action of the creative arts therapies: The psychodynamic model. *Arts in Psychotherapy Journal, 25* (2), 85–99.

Josselson, R. (2000). Relationships as a path to integrity, wisdom and meaning. In P. Young-Eisendrath & M. E. Miller (Eds.), *Psychology of mature spirituality* (pp. 87–102). London: Routledge.

Jourard, S. M. (1974). *Healthy personality*. New York: Macmillan.

Kalmanowitz, D., & Lloyd, B. (1999). Art therapy in the former Yugoslavia. *Arts in Psychotherapy Journal, 26* (1), 15–25.

Kohut, H. (1977). *The restoration of the self.* New York: International Universities Press.

Kohut, H. (1980). Two letters. In A. Goldberg (Ed.), *Advances in self psychology.* New York: International Universities Press.

Kubie, L. (1961). *Neurotic distortion of the creative process.* New York: Noonday Press.

Lahad, M. (1999). The use of drama therapy with crisis intervention groups, following mass evacuation. *The Arts in Psychotherapy Journal, 26* (1), 27–33.

Landy, R. (1997a). Introduction to special issue on the state of the arts. *Arts in Psychotherapy Journal, 24* (1), 3–4.

Landy, R. (1997b). Drama therapy—the state of the art. *Arts in Psychotherapy Journal, 24* (1), 5–15.

Langer, S. K. (1953). *Feeling and form: A theory of art.* New York: Charles Scribner's Sons.

Lerner, A. (1997). A look at poetry therapy. *Arts in Psychotherapy Journal, 24* (1), 81–89.

Lowen, A. (1970). The body in therapy. *American Dance Therapy Association Proceedings,* pp. 1–9.

Mahler, M., Pine, F., & Bergman, A. (1975). *The psychological birth of the human infant.* New York: Basic Books.

Main, M. (2000). The categories of infant, child and adult attachment. Flexible vs. inflexible attention under attachment related stress. *Journal of American Psychoanalytic Association, 48,* 1055–1096.

McNiff, S. (1997). Art therapy: A spectrum of partnerships. *Arts in Psychotherapy Journal, 24* (1), 37–44.

Miller, J. B. (1976). *Toward a new psychology of women.* Boston: Beacon Press.

Morgan, R. (2001). *The demon lover: The roots of terrorism.* New York: Washington Square Press.

Piaget, J. (1972). *Play, dreams and imitation in childhood.* New York: Norton.

Posada, G., & Jacobs, A. (2001). Child-mother attachment relationships and culture. *American Psychologist, 10,* 821–822.

Redmond, L. (1997). *When the drummers were women.* New York: Three Rivers Press.

Reich, W. (1949). *Character analysis.* New York: Farrar, Straus and Giroux.

Rogers, C. R. (1962). Toward a theory of creativity. In S. J. Parnes (Ed.), *A source book for creative thinking* (pp. 63–72). New York: Charles Scribner's Sons.

Rosenberg, K. R., & Trevathan, W. R. (2001, November). The evolution of human birth. *Scientific American,* pp. 72–77.

Rosenthal, R., Hall, J. A., Di Matteo, R., Rogers, P. L., & Archer, D. (1977).

Sensitivity to nonverbal communication. The PONS test. Unpublished monograph, Boston, MA: Harvard University.

Schuster, C. S., & Ashburn, S. S. (1992). *The process of human development: A holistic lifespan approach* (3rd ed.). Philadelphia: J.B. Lippincott.

Siegel, D. J. (1999). *The developing mind: Toward a neurobiology of interpersonal experience.* New York: Guildford Press.

Smilansky, S. (1968). *The effects of sociodramatic play in disadvantaged preschool children.* New York: Wiley.

Spitz, R. A. (1945). Hospitalism: An inquiry into the genesis of psychiatric conditions in early childhood. *Psychoanalytic Study of the Child, 1,* 53–74.

Stern, D. N. (1985). *The interpersonal world of the infant.* New York: Basic Books.

Stolorow, R. D., & Atwood, G. S. (1992). *Contexts of being: The intersubjective foundations of psychological life.* Hillsdale, NJ: The Analytic Press.

Sullivan, R. (2001, March 19). The 'charismatic adult.' What makes a child resilient? *Time,* p. 35.

Taylor, C. (1994). The politics of recognition. In D. T. Goldberg (Ed.), *Multiculturalism: A critical reader* (pp. 75–106). Malden, MA: Blackwell.

Terr, L. (1990). *Too scared to cry.* New York: Harper Collins.

Van Wagoner, S. L., Gelso, C. J., Hayes, J. A., & Diemer, R. A. (1991). Countertransference and the reputedly excellent therapist. *Psychotherapy: Theory, Research, Practice and Training, 28,* 411–421.

Walker, B. G. (1990). *Women's spirituality & ritual.* Gloucester, MA: Fair Winds Press.

Wallerstein, J. S., & Blakeslee, S. (1989). *Second chances.* Boston: Houghton Mifflin.

Winnicott, D. W. (1965). *The maturational processes and the facilitating environment.* New York: International Universities Press.

Winnicott, D. W. (1982). *Playing and reality.* New York: Penguin Books.

Young-Eisendrath, P., & Miller, M. E. (2000). *The psychology of mature spirituality.* London: Routledge.

Zwerling, I. (1989). The creative arts therapies as "Real Therapies." *American Dance Therapy Association Journal, 11* (1), 19–26.

CHAPTER 4

The Intimate Sphere: Site of Personal Artistic Expression and Self-Regeneration

Persons who are vulnerable to self-fragmentation because of the negative identifications and disturbed attachments they have formed during childhood, or who undergo a deep structural regression as a result of having been traumatized by catastrophic events over which they had little control, need to establish a reparative one-to-one relationship with a wise person who can help them make sense of their chaotic internal world, rapid shifts in consciousness and mood states, and metaphoric ways of communicating. By doing so, they can integrate these important experiences with their understanding of the consensual reality that is presented by others to recover their capacity to function more effectively in the outside world.

To accomplish the difficult task of self-integration and self-regeneration, creative arts therapists help set into motion three kinds of object relationships. The first is the internal subjective relationship that their clients establish with the illusory objects they create from their own experience and imagination, and transform into novel metaphors that possess the potential to alter their self and other perceptions. The second is the intersubjective relationship that clients co-construct with their therapist over time. This relationship allows clients to internalize functional aspects of the therapist that they need but lack. The internalization of functional aspects of the therapist helps clients to revise their self-narrative, construct a more coherent sense of self, and better regulate disruptive emotions. The third relationship is the interpersonal relationship that clients establish with their therapist or with members of a therapy group to which they belong. This relationship provides clients with an opportunity to understand how others actually perceive them, providing them with some sense of the norms of comportment and behavior that others in their society expect of them.

THE ILLUSORY OBJECT RELATIONSHIP

According to Jung (1961/1976, 1964), the most urgent need facing humanity is the discovery of the reality and value of one's active, symbolic inner life. A symbol is an image or a representation of something that is originally unknown, a mystery that exerts a powerful attraction and fascination for humans (Edinger, 1992). A symbol acts as a magnet of meaning, containing multiple meanings at once for an individual person or for a cultural group (Betsy, 1997). Describing the value of being able to connect with one's private, subjective self-experience, Estes (1995) commented:

Home is a sustained mood or sense that allows us to experience feelings not necessarily sustained in the mundane world.... The vehicles through which (we) reach home are many: music, art, forest, ocean, spume, sunrise, solitude. These take us home to a nutritive inner world that has ideas, order and sustenance all of its own (p. 307).

The inner symbolic life of human beings originates with the first illusory object that toddlers create from their own imagination. Winnicott (1982) used the term "transitional object" to refer to an object that becomes the toddler's first "not me" possession (p. 1). According to Winnicott (1982), a transitional object serves a critical soothing function for children by filling the terrifying void that they experience during the temporary absences of their primary caregiver.

In adulthood, the capacity to create illusory objects continues to find expression in the daydreams, night dreams, and other creative activities that adults generate spontaneously from their own experience and imagination. In the arts arena, these creative activities take the form of spontaneously created movement expressions, rhythmic sounds and melodies, visual objects, dramatic enactments, and poetic metaphors. Adults continue to engage in illusory object making to materially represent their symbolic inner life, to allay their fears and anxieties, and in part to fulfill their wishful fantasies. But, perhaps the most critical function that adults' continued capacity for illusion making and pretend playing serves for them is to support their capacity for self-regeneration through the reorganization of their self-experience and through the restoration of their emotional state of being to a more balanced state.

Early in the history of psychoanalysis, Freud (1911/1958) posited that art brought about a reconciliation between two regulating principles of mental functioning: pleasure and reality principles. He believed that under the pleasure principle, humans sought to achieve instant gratification through the experience of pleasure and the avoidance of unpleasure. In contrast, under the reality principle, humans sought to postpone instant gratification in favor of long-range gratification and self-preservation. He viewed the artist as someone who initially turned away from reality by refusing to renounce his instinctual satisfaction but then transformed the world of consensual reality for the better by making use of the insights that he gained from the world of fantasy.

[The artist is someone] who allows his erotic and ambitious wishes full play in the life of phantasy. He finds the way back to reality, however, from this world of phantasy by making use of special gifts to mold his phantasies into truths of a new kind, which are valued as precious reflections of reality (Freud, 1911, p. 224).

Four decades later, Kris (1952) pointed out that the creative process of illusory object making might be considered to be a form of regression in the service of the ego. Today, some contemporary psychoanalysts, including myself, view the creation of illusory objects as a type of object relationship as well as a site where self-transformation can take place:

The artist's relationship to his or her art is a type of object relationship, imbued with reality and fantasy, comparable to that between patient and analyst. In its self-object capacity, the work of art validates the artist's sense of effectance. It also has the potential to repair defective early relations and to strengthen one's ego and self-esteem (Knafo, 2002, p. 46).

In a paper I wrote recently, "Frida Kahlo: Self-other representation and self healing through art," I described the various self-healing functions that Frida Kahlo's artwork served for her (Dosamantes-Beaudry, 2001). Not only did the artist use her artwork to depict the psychodynamics that she had experienced in her relationships with significant others, but she also used her numerous self-portraits to secure an intact, undamaged, alikeness of herself to create a mirroring selfobject that she felt she lacked in childhood. In a follow-up paper, "Frida Kahlo: The creation of a cultural icon," I described how certain politically disenfranchised artists groups in this country subsequently came to appropriate the artist's image into their own artwork, not only to bolster their own self-esteem and social status as artists, but also to valorize their societally stigmatized cultural identities (Dosamantes-Beaudry, 2002).

For many adult clients, forging a relationship with the illusory objects that they create helps them to reconnect with their own potential to be creative. This relationship may feel safer than the intersubjective relationship that requires collaboration with their therapist. The latter relationship is experienced as more emotionally charged and fluid, and one they cannot readily control or manipulate at will. The relationship with an illusory object can therefore serve as an initial, intermediary selfobject relationship, providing the therapist and client with indirect clues about the client's internal world and the client's past and current attachments and identifications with others.

The subjective relationship that adults establish with the illusory objects that they create shares similar characteristics to those that Winnicott (1982) attributed to children's first transitional object relationship, namely: (a) the children exert sole possession and control over the illusory object that they create, (b) the self-object that they create can be loved or mutilated by them, (c) this illusory object provides comfort and possesses a powerful, magical attraction for them, and (d) it is neither mourned nor forgotten by them, but, with time, simply loses its meaning for them (Winnicott, 1982, pp. 5–6). The subsequent metaphors that adult clients derive from the symbolic, illusory selfobject relationship that they create provide them with a verbal handle with which to unravel the personal meaning these objects hold for them when cast within the framework of their past as well as current relationships, including the relationship that they construct with their therapist in the present.

THE CONSTRUCTION OF A SENSE OF SELF AND THE THERAPEUTIC INTERSUBJECTIVE RELATIONSHIP

The term self refers to a psychological structure that, through experience, comes to acquire coherence and continuity, and, with time, assumes a characteristic shape and organization (Stolorow, Brandchaft, & Atwood, 1987). In most cultures, the mother serves as the initial and primary carrier of her child's cultural worldview. The development of a cognitive sense of self originates and is preceded by the somatic acquisition of a sense of self (Dosamantes-Beaudry, 1997b; Krueger, 1989). The cultural worldview that a mother provides her offspring is internalized somatically by them. Through their construction of a body sense, infants begin to take the first monumental step toward creating a sense of self that reflects their cultural worldview (Dosamantes-Beaudry, 1997a). This sense of one's body self is acquired through a sequence of bodily kinds of experiences that allow children to differentiate self from nonself and interior from exterior, and to gradually internalize a bodily appearance that is congruent with the standards of beauty and comportment set by their society.

The kind of self that is likely to be constructed among traditional cultures is one that emphasizes the interdependence of all things and the fusion of ordinary with extraordinary reality, encompasses multiple components with permeable boundaries, holds a contiguous sense of time, and is linked to others' welfare and points of view. In contrast, the kind of self that is likely to be constructed by members of Western, modernist cultures who value individualism, independence, and the discreteness of things and active states of consciousness, is a solitary, discrete self with bounded boundaries and a discrete sense of time and sense of agency (Dosamantes-Beaudry, 1997a). The possession of a strong, personal sense of self appears to be a critical factor in a Western person's ability to cope with unpredictable and stressful circumstances as an individual.

Contemporary psychoanalytic theory has much to offer to a Western, modernist construction of a sense of self, one that is mediated within the intimate sphere of social relationships that a person forges with caregivers and, later, with other significant persons. The founder of attachment theory, Bowlby (1984), was optimistic about the capability of psychoanalytic therapy to modify a person's early attachment patterns. According to Neborsky (2002), Bowlby did not view patients as helpless victims of powerful unconscious drives that created unbearable conflicts and defenses, but instead considered the need for social emotional safety, security, and comfort to be the cornerstone of mental health. This principle also guides the direction of contemporary attachment research, which examines the kinds of attachment styles individuals forge during childhood and later replicate with others, including their therapist.

OBJECT RELATIONS THEORY AND SELF-ORGANIZATION

During the latter part of the twentieth century, psychoanalytic research began to shift its focus away from drive theories toward theories that focused on the impact that significant social relationships have upon the construction of a person's self-psychological structure and subjective representation of self and other relationships (Kernberg, 1976; Stolorow & Lachman, 1980).

Object relations theory is a psychoanalytic theory that is concerned with how a person transforms interpersonal relationships into subjective, internal mental representations of self and others in action. From an object relations perspective, the self is viewed as an evolving subjective center of a person's personality that evolves through active and evermore complex interactions with significant others, becoming an increasingly more differentiated psychic entity by the slow and gradual process of individuation (Kernberg, 1976; Mahler, Pine, & Bergman, 1975).

From an object relations perspective, clients are viewed as having achieved a particular level of emotional self-other differentiation. In adulthood they transfer these same characteristics and patterns onto significant others, including their therapist (Hedges, 1983). Clients whose emotional development has become inflexibly set before they have had an opportunity to achieve object constancy[1] will experience and communicate with their therapist in strikingly different ways from those clients who have been able to achieve object constancy, who possess greater emotional flexibility, and who have a wider range of emotional expressiveness.

At the earliest or first level of emotional self-other differentiation, one experiences others in terms of part-objects in an inconstant "self-other matrix" (Hedges, 1983). One's self-organization occurs around part-objects that interact with other part-objects in unpredictable ways that are beyond one's ability to comprehend or to control. (For instance, in chapter 2, Mary Barnes's description of the regressive state that she reached while undergoing a downward emotional spiral exemplifies the kind of subjective experience of a person who functions emotionally at a diffuse and fragmented level of self-other differentiation.)

The second level of self-other differentiation is characterized by one's experience of others in terms of a merger or a literal sense of oneness with one's environment or others. This level corresponds to Mahler et al.'s (1975) symbiotic phase of emotional development. (A dance/movement therapy client with whom I worked in a closed ward of a mental hospital provides an example of this level of self-other differentiation. This young woman very rapidly developed an intense, indiscriminate, positive attachment to me. During her therapy sessions, she would panic whenever she would close her eyes, and she would attempt to move spontaneously on her own initiative. She dreaded this experience because when she closed her eyes she would lose all contact with her own physical boundaries, and this meant to her that she and I had ceased to exist.)

The third level of self-other differentiation is achieved when others are recognized as separate beings from one's self, but still are treated as functional aspects of one's self, to cope adequately with the outside world. (A client with whom I worked privately through dance/movement therapy provides an example of this level of self-other differentiation. Whenever she became panicked in a social situation outside of the therapeutic arena, she would need to conjure up an image of me addressing her in a calm and serene manner to quiet herself down. Her repeated enactment of this fantasy in other social contexts indicated to me that she had not yet internalized the capacity to soothe herself during my absence and still needed to resort to the use of an imaginary, auxiliary ego to function adequately on her own.)

At the fourth level of self-other differentiation, one is able to recognize and tolerate others' psychological distinctiveness and separateness by acknowledging through one's actions that others possess their own centers of initiative and have independent needs and motives of their own that may differ from one's own. (A client whom I saw in private practice, who had been physically abused as a child, used to enjoy enacting her own sadistic fantasies toward all authority figures, including me. She did so by continually referring to me as her "toilet mother" into whom she "could dump (her) crap." Toward the end of our work together, however, this client became capable of acknowledging "being grateful" to me "for having contained her rage" and for not having retaliated in kind. Her reparative gesture informed me that she was now able to take responsibility for her own rageful behavior, and she could actually perceive me as someone who could be hurt and who possessed independent needs of my own.)

According to Klein (1975), the experience of gratitude is essential to one's development of appreciation in the goodness of one's self and others:

Gratitude is closely bound up with generosity. Inner wealth derives from having assimilated the good object so that the individual becomes able to share its gifts with others. This makes it possible to introject a more friendly outer world, and a feeling of enrichment ensues (p. 189).

Although the various levels of self-other differentiation described earlier serve as a useful guideline for determining a client's self-state in relation to others, it is important to remember that each person lives within an intersubjective world that is uniquely and idiosyncratically his or her own. This intersubjective world is fluid, multidimensional, and context driven. It is a subjective world that is colored by the personal and cultural symbols that are drawn from each person's own personal and cultural history (Orange, 1992).

Kohut (1984) coined the term "transmuting internalization" to refer to the process whereby clients come to appropriate particular psychological attributes that are modelled by their therapist to bolster their own tenuous sense of self and to function more effectively in the outside world (p. 99). Self psychologists use the term selfobject to refer to the supportive psychological functions that therapists serve for clients who have not yet been able to achieve a coherent and stable sense of self.

The process of transmuting internalization begins when clients begin to replicate or imitate in action, outside of the therapeutic arena, those therapist functions that they need but cannot yet provide for themselves. Piaget (1967) referred to behavior that is initially imitated during the absence of the person being imitated as "replicated action." Through such replicated action or deferred imitation, clients begin to emulate in action particular functions that they associate with their therapist, outside of the therapeutic arena. The following are examples of how some of the clients I have worked with have made use of deferred imitation as an intermediary step, prior to their being able to spontaneously and automatically perform these actions for themselves:

One client mentioned that whenever she felt anxious, she would rock gently while imagining herself being gently and securely rocked by me. This deferred imitative behavior helped to soothe her and enabled her to become calm.

A second client reported that whenever she became anxious outside of the therapeutic arena, she smiled in the same way that she recalled me doing during our sessions together. By imitating my behavior in other social contexts, she was able to quiet herself down.

A third client mentioned that whenever she felt negative, unpleasant emotions, she would visualize me and then herself as a safe deposit box, capable of containing those emotions that she found very difficult to tolerate within herself (Dosamantes-Alperson, 1985). Holding this image allowed her to kinesthetically identify with the experience of letting herself become a container for such "bad feelings."

When clients are able to automatically perform needed psychological functions without first having to resort to such deferred imitative actions, one can assume that they have internalized these functions and have succeeded in making them their own. Among the kinds of self-psychological functions that clients come to appropriate, internalize, and spontaneously perform over time are the abilities (a) to organize their self-experience, (b) to soothe themselves when anxious, (c) to act as mirroring selfobjects for themselves, (d) to tolerate and better regulate the disruptive emotions they experience, (e) to modulate the expression of their impulses, (f) to widen their expressive response repertoire and to become more flexible and spontaneous, (g) to reclaim shadow aspects of themselves that previously they projected onto others, (h) to heal the internal splits that resulted from their denial of negative self-experience, and (i) to experience and demonstrate genuine concern and empathy for themselves and others.

THE RELATIONAL CONTEXT OF CREATIVE ARTS THERAPIES

Creative arts therapists whose therapeutic work is informed by contemporary psychoanalytic theory are able to adopt a listening and attending posture that is emotionally attuned to their particular client's shifting emotional states and levels of self-other differentiation (Hedges, 1983). Within the safe potential space facilitated by a creative arts therapist, clients can begin to forge the three kinds of object relationships that were described at the beginning of this chapter. The first is the illusory relationship that they create with objects, symbols, and metaphors that they derive from their own experience and active imagination. The second is the intersubjective relationship they weave between themselves and their therapist. The third is the interpersonal relationship they establish with their therapist or with members of a therapy group. In combination, these three kinds of relationships help to reorganize clients' internal self-experience and to strengthen their self-esteem and sense of effectiveness in the world, which, in turn, enable them to successfully negotiate the difficult developmental and situational challenges that they face.

When coping with difficult developmental or external transitions, the first phase of the transition process centers around the establishment of a safe psychological environment and the creation of potential space. The second phase of the transition process begins when clients are able to trust the intersubjective relationship they have established with their therapist and feel free to voluntarily regress and begin to generate new associations to old object relationships via an art-making process that engages them in the use of spontaneous gestures and movements, rhythms and sounds, material and imaginary objects, dramatic enactments, and verbal metaphors. During the third phase of the transition process, clients begin to work through the current meaning of the problematic issues that they raised during the second phase. It is important to note that clients appear to repeat the second and third phases of the transition process numerous times during the course of therapy in cyclical fashion, until they experience the process to be completed.

In the next section of this chapter, several case vignettes help to illustrate how some creative arts therapies clients learned to mediate the difficult developmental challenges they encountered in their lives.

REORGANIZING SELF-EXPERIENCE THROUGH THE CREATION OF ILLUSORY SELFOBJECT RELATIONSHIPS

Jean Davis (1999) is an art therapist at a women's homeless shelter in Brooklyn, New York. The Transitional Community (TLC) Program that sponsored her art therapy work and helps homeless women with a history of five or more hospitalizations find permanent housing. Most of the residents at the shelter have histories of physical, sexual, and substance abuse.

Davis (1999) spearheaded an art-making project that involved the building of a community sculpture park in an empty lot outside of the shelter that had been leased to the TLC Program. She mobilized her clients' involvement with her project by encouraging their participation in a scavenger hunt. Residents began to dig the lot in search of scraps and objects that they might use as structural materials in the construction of their own community park sculptures. In the lot, they found all sorts of part objects such as parts of kitchen equipment, tiles, bricks, stuffed animals, dolls, and syringes. As they dug, they became engaged in dialogues about who might have previously inhabited the grounds and for what purposes the grounds might be currently used.

Davis (1999) describes the intentions of her art therapy project in the following way:

Many of our clients, much like the vacant lots, also have histories tainted from a life of substance abuse, destruction and loss. But like the treasures found in the

Photo 4.1   *Never Ending Journey.* Copyright, Jean Davis, M.P.S., ATR-BC, art therapist.

vacant lots, the internal make up of these ladies can also be seen as a space full of possibilities to build. Perhaps with some attachment, hard work and creativity, some clients would develop a center, core or an ego (p. 47).

One resident who created her first sculpture for the community park began by collecting particular objects that she decided to include in her sculpture: an old subway handrail, a few small stairs, and a concrete owl. She reconstructed, painted, and arranged these items into a sculpted piece that she named *Never Ending Journey* (see Photo 4.1). While creating her sculpture, the resident offered several spontaneous explanations regarding the meaning that she attached to its various components. Apparently, the handrail and stairs led her to the name that she chose for the piece. To her the owl offered light, hope, and protection, and came to represent for her those functional aspects of her therapist that she herself lacked.

In describing the meaning that the owl held for this resident at this point in the art-making process, Davis (1999) commented that "[this resident] like many of the women of the shelter, has very little—if any— sense of self. The only identification [she] can take is in the owl with the light" (p. 47). Gradually, the homeless shelter resident began to create a central figure, a woman. By creating this woman, she was symbolically representing what she needed to do for herself (i.e., to reconstruct a core sense of herself).

In her therapeutic work, Davis (1999) seems to have been guided by several metaphors. The metaphor of the scavenger hunt became an analogy for "going on an archeological dig," where residents could be encouraged to dig for buried treasure for the purpose of uncovering significant clues about their own past and to reveal something about their current and future potential (p. 46). Davis's project was also guided by the metaphor of "building from scraps" to refer to the gradual self-reconstruction that shelter residents underwent through the illusory object relationships they established with the shards and pieces of discarded objects that they found in the lot and selected for their artwork (p. 45).

Davis's (1999) community sculpture park project for homeless shelter residents showed how an art-making process that actively engaged shelter residents helped them to convert an empty lot into a site for self-transformation. At this site, residents were able to construct selfobject relationships with those objects that they found in their environment and held a strong, personal emotional connection for them. According to Knafo (2002), an art-making process offers the creator both an opportunity to seek objects and an opportunity to reenact a reunion with the found objects.

Davis's (1999) art-making project lends support to the notion that what is external and material often reflects what is less obvious, internal, and ephemeral, and that, under the facilitative conditions provided by an effective creative arts therapist, clients can actively search their environment for objects or symbols that best represent their own subjective, internal symbolic experience. In turn, these external representations can help make the invisible visible, and what was previously unconscious or preconscious can be given a material existence.

ENACTING AND REGULATING PRIMAL SELF-STATES

In childhood, pretend role-playing offers children an opportunity to make predictions about others' actions and thoughts (Azar, 2002). Through pretend play, children have an opportunity to practice the art of simulation. They can simulate what other persons may be thinking and feeling. Drama therapists view the concept of self as one involving a complex role system that a person can tap into to achieve mastery over difficult challenges (Landy, 1994).

Craig Haen and Kenneth Brannon (2002) are two drama therapists who conduct drama therapy groups with latency-aged boys at a residential treatment facility in White Plains, New York. These boys all have histories of abuse, neglect, and abandonment. They come from families in which parental drug abuse, domestic violence, and emotional dysfunction are pervasive. According to Haen and Brannon, before their participation in drama therapy groups, these boys lacked access to certain kinds of psychological functions:

[They] are often unable to harness their impulses and to modulate their emotions. Their reactions to external stimuli are quite primitive, and their boundaries are in constant flux. The boys have tremendous difficulty in negotiating interpersonal relationships (Haen & Brannon, p. 31).

However, within the safe holding environment provided by Haen and Brannon (2002), the boys became engaged in role-playing certain dramatic characters and stories that reflected some connection to their own subjective experience. Through the roles they elected to enact, the boys gave their therapists clues about their "interior landscape" and about "the dynamics of the group as a whole" (p. 32). The therapeutic goals set by Haen and Brannon for their clients included the expansion of each boy's role repertoire, the boys' increased tolerance for ambivalent emotional reactions, and the boys' increased capacity to organize and make coherent the fragments of their self-experience.

As a group, these boys preferred to enact three roles in particular: superhero, monster, and baby. The boys' attraction to the role of superhero was best exemplified by their choice of Superman. Their attraction to this superhero can be explained by the fact that Superman simultaneously holds two opposing kinds of self-states with which the boys could readily identify. By assuming the role of Clark Kent, they were able to identify with this character's social ineptness and awkwardness, and by assuming the role of Superman, they were able to identify with this character's strength and omnipotence.

Those boys who were drawn to the role of the monster seemed to have especially strong needs for attention and recognition. They enjoyed enacting the monstrous and bestial qualities of the monster character because their actions got them the attention and recognition that they longed for from authority figures and from their peers. Within the context of these groups, the boys who chose to role-play being monsters were free to enact their raw, destructive impulses and then to try on new alternative behaviors that were suggested to them by their therapists and peers. By trying on new alternative actions, the boys learned to transform their primal reactions into more socially acceptable reactions.

The role of the baby seems to have been preferred by those boys who had been seriously emotionally deprived and who had experienced themselves as being extremely vulnerable. When the boys' emotional needs were temporarily frustrated, they became enraged with Haen and Brannon (2002), who modelled for them how to act as containers for the boys' raw emotions. Then they helped the boys find alternative ways to gratify their needs for attention and nurturance in more age-appropriate ways.

For instance, by enacting "saving the baby" or by "caring for the baby," these emotionally deprived boys learned to symbolically take care of themselves.

Haen and Brannon (2002) summarize the impact that the drama therapy groups they conducted had upon the emotionally deprived and abused latency-aged boys with whom they work as follows:

In working with the roles of superhero, monster and baby, we watched our clients expand their relatedness, their ability to express and to contain powerful affect, their cohesiveness as a group and their ability to access inner strengths (p. 39).

The therapeutic work of art therapist Jean Davis (1999) and drama therapists Craig Haen and Kenneth Brennon (2002) offer fine examples of how creative arts therapists who provide supportive, predictable, playful potential spaces and serve as "good enough" emotional containers for their clients can succeed in facilitating their clients' engagement in the serious pretend playing that ultimately results in their clients' ability to reorganize their symbolic self-experience.

BOLSTERING COPING MECHANISMS AND RESTORING SELF-MASTERY

With clients who are particularly fragile and vulnerable, such as those who face a life-threatening illness, sometimes the most healing thing a therapist can do is to help them fortify whatever resources and coping mechanisms they have available to them, so that they can continue to carry on with life in the most optimal way possible. For instance, children who suffer from certain hematological or oncological diseases for which they must undergo bone marrow transplantation are placed in the difficult position of having to respond to potentially life-threatening conditions over which they have little control; face their fear of dying; and suffer the insult of bodily disfigurement, social isolation, and abandonment. It is not surprising, therefore, that these children's initial reaction to their illness is shock, denial, and outward compliance with the medical treatment that they receive (Gunter, 2000). However, when their brittle defenses collapse, they undergo an involuntarily regression. As they regress, they are likely to become agitated, throw temper tantrums, become depressed, retreat from others, and refuse to cooperate with their medical treatment.

Adults who suffer from potentially life-threatening illnesses, such as breast cancer, not only have to deal with the fear of dying and the negative side effects generated by the chemotherapy treatments that they receive, but, in the case of women patients, they also have to contend with the toll of having a visible and socially valued part of their bodies amputated and, in most instances, with the trauma of having to undergo additional reconstructive surgery (Borgmann, 2002). Like the children who undergo bone marrow transplantation, these adult medical patients also feel socially isolated and abandoned because frequently members of their own families find it difficult to handle their reactions to a loved one's illness and, therefore, fail to provide the kind of social support a seriously ill person needs. In light of such monumental self-losses (diminished social power, loss of control over one's body, loss of self-esteem, sudden and drastic body image changes, and reduced social relatedness), it is not surprising that many adult women patients who are diagnosed with breast cancer become extremely depressed and experience poor interpersonal functioning for at least an entire year following their diagnosis.

Artistic expression seems to offer seriously ill persons who are undergoing medical treatment for life-threatening conditions a way to obtain the understanding and emotional support they need from a wise and nonintrusive adult to cope with their condition. When physically ill patients work with a creative arts therapist, they are able to communicate about their self-experience through an intermediate selfobject that allows them to organize their unspeakable emotions and thoughts and, over time, to acquire some sense of mastery over the difficult circumstances that they face but cannot control.

Most terminally ill persons know that they are dying whether or not they have been told. What a dying person seems to fear most is the anticipated pain of the dying process and abandonment of any type (Schuster & Ashburn, 1992). Kubler-Ross (1969) claimed that most dying persons passed through five stages of grieving in anticipation of their death: (a) denial and isolation, (b) anger, (c) bargaining, (d) depression, and (e) acceptance. Although no two persons face death in identical ways, it is the case that, without open communication, effective coping on the part of both the living and the dying becomes much more difficult (Schuster & Ashburn, 1992).

Janette Farrell Fenton (2000) is an art therapist who works with non-hospitalized children who have been diagnosed with cystic fibrosis (a) genetic disease that can have serious effects on multiple systems of the body and can lead to life-threatening conditions). She contends that for these children, "art-making can promote feelings of self esteem, and improved body image, lessen feelings of isolation and synthesize spoken and unspoken fears" (p. 17).

Fenton (2000) notes that children who are affected by this disease often exhibit a powerful need to create and to "leave a trace" of themselves in the face of an unknown future (p. 22). The strength of such a life-asserting wish can be observed in one of her adolescent patient's, John, who at the age of 15 years had to be hospitalized for liver failure. Before he passed away, he spontaneously created a drawing he called *John's World* (see Photo 4.2).

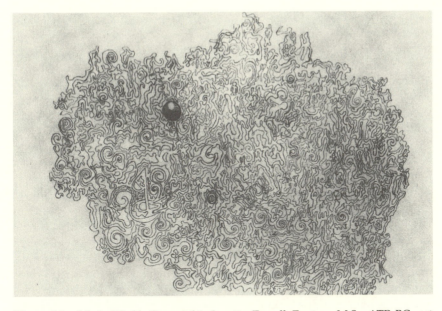

Photo 4.2 *John's World.* Copyright, Janette Farrell Fenton, M.S., ATR-BC, art therapist.

In describing John's drawing, Fenton (2000) observed that John's world consisted of "a world of imagery, as animals, human figures, suns and sailboats co-mingle with the camouflaged letters of his name. It is as if he wishes to leave traces of self in the artwork" (p. 22).

THE RECOVERY OF PREVERBAL MEMORIES

Before the advent of language, the body is the theater in which distress gets played out (McDougall, 1989). Raphael-Leff (1994) has observed that a caregiver's body language and silent encounters often become absorbed in the body image of her child as unconscious images or as an affective commentary upon her child's self. Krueger (1989) contends that early somatic disruptions before a stable, integrated cohesive body image has been established are likely to be the result of either overly intrusive, emotionally unavailable or selective caregiver responses. For instance, children who have had overly intrusive caregivers learn to resort to such protective coping strategies as dissociation, splitting, depersonalization, withdrawal, and numbing as a way to create a stimulus barrier and to avoid physical intimacy.

The value of being able to perceive and to express ourselves somatically and imagistically can best be illustrated through the experiences of persons who have been exposed to traumatic events before they have had an opportunity to acquire the use of language. Sometimes the first inkling that an adult has that such an event has actually taken place is through the experience of some disturbing, yet persistent, somatic symptom for which no medical explanation or treatment can be found. Under such circumstances, the possibility that the somatic symptom itself may represent an implicit somatic recollection that has not yet been assimilated by the person has to be considered.

According to Siegel (2001), the autobiographical narrative that a person creates about her self-experience seems to be influenced directly by early, nonverbal, implicit memories and later by verbal, more explicit memories. Humans' implicit memory is intact from birth, whereas semantic memory begins to function at about the age of two years. Implicit memory involves parts of the brain that do not require conscious processing during encoding or retrieval (Squire, 1987). Under ordinary circumstances, the experience of childhood amnesia does not have to be attributed to any kind of impairment because before the age of five years, the consolidation process that transforms short-term memory into permanent memory is not yet mature. However, in instances in which an infant has actually been exposed to a traumatic event or a series of repeated traumatic events that involve a parent who engages in abusive or frightening behavior, the child is faced with the paradoxical experience of being terrified by the very person who is supposed to be the source of his or her safety and comfort (Main, 1999). Siegel (2001) contends that persons who carry such unresolved traumatic memories may suffer from an impairment in the cortical consolidation process that leaves the memories of such events out of reach of permanent, explicit memory. Such unresolved tension states can then disrupt the normal integrative functioning of the person and cause the person to resort to perseverative responses that inhibit her or his development of a coherent sense of self.

The following case vignette of an adult woman who was a client of mine in private dance/movement therapy traces the therapeutic process that facilitated her explicit recall of a repeated traumatic event that took place before she learned to speak.

As the first phase of our dance/movement therapy work was coming to an end and a sense of mutual trust as well as trust in the experiential movement process itself had begun to be established, Emily, who was 34 years old, began to move into phases two and three of a transitional healing process. This shift occurred one day when she spontaneously mentioned that "ever since (she) could remember (she) needed to evacuate frequently whenever (she) became anxious" and that the physicians whom she had consulted about her problem "had found no physical reasons to account for it." All she knew was that whenever she became anxious, she would "experience an urgent need to evacuate for no apparent reason." She referred to her problem as one involving her "irritable bowel."

Emily began her movement work by closing her eyes and focusing on the bodily-felt sensation that she experienced in her irritable bowel. She described the sensations that she experienced in this part of her as "hot" and "red." As she identified through receptive movement with the physical sensation of "hot" and the image of "red," she began to move in the way that she experienced each of these sensory qualities.

(In psychoanalytically informed dance/movement therapy, clients are able to make direct contact with their own bodily-felt experience by connecting receptively to their somatic self-experience. By closing their eyes and attending inwardly, their focus automatically shifts from an active to a receptive state of awareness. While in a receptive state, they are able to conjure internal bodily-felt and imagistic associations to the problematic situations that they face [Dosamantes-Alperson, 1979; Dosamantes-Beaudry, 1999]. When they can recover the sensations and bodily images that are associated with these situations, they can further differentiate the meaning that these situations hold for them in the present.)

As Emily began to move each quality of her somatic symptom, she laid on the floor on one side of her body in a curled up position. Her entire body then suddenly began to contract and spasm until she gradually became very still. She then rose to standing. As she did so, her chest expanded and her movement became more outer directed. As her movement began to gather momentum, it assumed a distinctively more violent form—she used her arms and hands to slash and cut through the air. When she stopped moving, her movement experience became crystallized into a single movement metaphor: "my pain-rage dance."

At our next session, Emily was eager to resume the sensory exploration that she had initiated during the previous session. She sat down, quieted herself down, and closed her eyes. Then, as she began to reflect upon the "pain-rage" metaphor that had emerged from her experience of the previous session, a spontaneous visual image of a witch-like figure appeared to her. Soon the witch image became transformed into an image of her own mother. Her mother appeared to be reaching into an infant's anal cavity and to be extracting some fecal matter with her hand. As she recounted this experience to me, Emily became aware of an urgent need to evacuate. It was as if the pieces of a puzzle were gradually coming into place to reveal something that she could not have discovered solely through words.

At our next session, Emily recounted that after her last session, she had telephoned her mother who lived in another state to confirm the validity of her imaged recollection. Her mother readily acknowledged that when Emily was an infant, she had regularly reached into her anal cavity to empty its fecal contents because she had found this child-rearing practice to be an efficient way "to keep Emily's interior clean." Her mother did not seem to experience her behavior as ego dystonic in any way, but simply saw her actions as a testament to her having been "a conscientious mother" whose primary concern had been for "her daughter's personal hygiene." When Emily recounted her phone conversation to me, I inquired whether, during our work together, there may not have been times when

she experienced me as "robbing her of her innermost thoughts?" Although she
laughed and dismissed my question as "silly," she did confirm that there had been
times in the past when she "had resented having to explore certain things deeply
when (she) would rather have avoided them altogether."

Once the implicit memory associated with Emily's somatic symptom was made
explicit and she was able to recover the relational component that the repeated
traumatic event she had experienced as a child held for her, she was now able to
get in touch with how helpless she might have felt as an infant during those times
when her mother had invaded the interior of her body space. Having had no
words with which to object to her mother's ministrations, her urge to evacuate
apparently remained her sole means of recalling the painful event. In adulthood
her urge to evacuate seemed to be always triggered whenever she felt helpless
and resistive toward other people's intrusions. As an adult, she was now able to
perceive her own bodily reactions and somatic perceptions as important information about the emotional tenor of her personal relationships, and therefore to
have more options about how to respond to perceived intrusiveness by others.
Within the therapeutic relationship, Emily also began to express negative emotions
more freely than she had in the past and to reclaim shadow aspects of herself,
such as her rage, which previously she had not been able to acknowledge.

By directly contacting her somatic symptom through the enactive and
imagistic modes in which it was originally expressed, Emily was able to
retrieve the recollection of a preverbally experienced traumatic event that
made it possible for her to acknowledge her current resentment and resistance toward the emotional uncovering and deepening process that is
a part of a psychodynamic therapeutic process. Being able to acknowledge
her infantile rage within the psychological safety of the therapeutic relationship, feelings that Emily had considered to be unseemly in the past,
could now be reclaimed by her.

THE SOMATIC DIALOGUE OF THE
INTERSUBJECTIVE RELATIONSHIP

A major aspect of the intersubjective relationship that evolves between
a therapist and her client is the unfolding of the somatic and nonverbal
exchange that takes place between both participants, or the *somatic intersubjective dialogue* (Dosamantes-Beaudry, 1997b). This concept seems appropriate when describing the overall nature of the somatic relationship
that exists at any given moment between a therapist and her client.
Whereas the term *somatic transference* seems more appropriate when attending only to the somatic reactions of the client toward the therapist,
the term *somatic countertransference* appears to be more appropriate when
referring solely to the somatic reactions that the therapist has toward the
client.

The somatic intersubjective dialogue is a critical feature of psychoanalytically informed dance/movement therapy (Dosamantes-Beaudry, 1999). In this form of dance/movement therapy, special attention is given by the therapist to her own bodily-felt reactions while simultaneously attending and tracking the emotional tenor and potential meaning contained in the client's enacted movement metaphors. Being able to track the ongoing somatic dialogue is critical, even for verbal psychotherapists who work within the traditional framework of psychoanalysis, which relies heavily upon the analysand's verbal free associations and the verbal interpretations made by the psychoanalyst. The value of being able to systematically track the somatic dialogue, and the somatic transference and countertransference reactions of the analysand and the analyst, will be demonstrated with a psychoanalytic analysand who was engaged in negotiating the difficult developmental transition of structural self-regeneration.

The psychoanalytic process to be described illustrates the intense emotional shifts that a middle-aged analysand with a history of emotional abandonment and physical abuse enacted while actively engaged in an ongoing intersubjective psychoanalytic relationship with me. These sessions demonstrate how she projected onto me early traumatic events that she originally experienced with her parents. The sessions also show how I tracked the various somatic components of the evolving therapeutic intersubjective relationship to contain her rage, so that it could be processed and fed back to her in a more benign form, thereby generating a reparative or healing impact upon her (Dosamantes-Beaudry, 1997b). The sessions to be described took place following the first vacation break I took from our work together:

When I returned Ellen insisted upon total silence. Any sound I made provoked a strong negative reaction from her. She would place her hands over her ears to indicate that I was intruding unbearably into the pristine silence of her solitude. At the end of each of several sessions, she walked out without saying a single word to me. Despite the lack of verbal exchange permitted by her, the vivid images her imposed silence generated in me, enabled me to track the emotional tone of the intersubjective relationship that was unfolding between us. Initially, a constrictive feeling in my throat and chest gave way to an image of myself as her hostage being choked to death by her. However, towards the end of the two week period (the exact time I had been away on vacation), I began to relax and to breathe more easily and the image of being choked to death gave way to a more benign one. I visualized myself as pregnant; holding her as a neonate in my womb while rocking in a comfortable chair. It seemed that the rageful baby had been soothed and transformed into a more tranquil albeit still unformed fetus. With the last image, the phrase "born again" came to mind. Although she continued to insist that I not speak, my whole body eased into a tranquil, relaxed state. I took the shift in my body sense and images to mean that probably a similar shift had taken place in her; that her vindictive rage had temporarily subsided and given way to a more tolerable holding space. It was at this juncture that I was able to verbally interpret her silence without encountering any objection from her. I said "how ex-cruciatingly painful it must be to feel abandoned and to be reminded that we each lead separate lives." Ellen cried quietly without uttering a word (pp. 525–526).

RESURRECTING AN EMBODIED, PLAYFUL, VITAL SELF

Sometimes people who are exposed to a sudden, traumatic event also undergo a rapid structural regression as a way of coping with the over-whelming emotional overload that they experience. The next case to be presented is that of a young woman who had been an active member of a long-term dance/movement therapy group. Although she had achieved object constancy and functioned at a higher level of self-other differenti-ation than the clients described earlier by Davis (1999) and Haen and Brannon (2002) in their work, when she became the unfortunate victim of two violent physical attacks, she temporarily involuntarily regressed to an earlier symbiotic level of emotional development. Members of her group realized that, as a group, they had a crisis situation on their hands, and they selflessly elected to make Crystal's healing process the focal point for the entire group. Although the group continued to function and group members continued to address issues that were of concern to each of them, Crystal's healing process dominated most of the group's attention for an entire year. The arts-based healing process that she moved through during this time helped to restore her to a more integrated state.

Crystal, 24 years old, was a member of a long-term dance/movement therapy group that I conducted with 12 women who ranged in age from 21 to 36 years and who varied with respect to racial and ethnic identity. The women were vol-unteers who were interested in exploring themselves through a therapeutic movement process. The group met twice weekly for two-hour long sessions. The group was open-ended and focused on the individual and group dynamics of the participants.

The group had been running for about one year when Crystal showed up one day to the group looking unkempt and in shock, as though she might have been the untoward victim of a bad car accident. She had bruises throughout her body. She reported that a neighbor whom she had known casually had knocked at the door of her apartment, where she lived with her husband (the latter happened to be away at work). The young man initiated a conversation with her and then, suddenly without warning, held her at knifepoint and proceeded to rape her. Fearing for her life, she had complied with his directives. After the rape, he asked her for her car keys and proceeded to tape her mouth, hands, and feet. He then took the keys of her car and stowed her into the trunk of her car and drove away from her neighborhood. She feared that, unless she found a way to free herself and to escape, he would likely kill her and abandon her body at some inaccessible terrain where her husband and the authorities would never be able to find her. While trapped in the trunk of her car, she managed to tear the tape off of her body and to click open the trunk of her car from the inside, so that when her assailant stopped at a gas station to get some cigarettes, she ran away toward a well-lit street. She found a pay phone, dialed 911 for help, and then phoned her husband at home. Because the assailant was driving her car, the police were able capture him almost immediately by using the license plate of her car as a means of identification. The police took her to a hospital, where she underwent a thorough physical examination and was questioned by a rape counselor.

Upon hearing her story, all members of the group offered her the unconditional support of the group. They offered to make her healing process a top priority for the group. What follows is a summary of the healing process that was transacted by her with other group members.

For many weeks, Crystal laid quietly under a large blanket that she had brought from home. This blanket had been a prized possession of hers since childhood. She referred to it as "my security blanket." Because she made it clear to the group that she simply wanted to lay quietly and undisturbed, initially the group went on with the group's work while continuing nonverbally to monitor Crystal's actions. As the group went on, two or three members of the group spontaneously began to create "a vigil circle" around Crystal. Several group members took turns serving in this capacity. As the group continued, so did Crystal's self-imposed hibernation.

During this period, what seemed to be of importance to group members was their desire to communicate to Crystal that they were there to provide a secure and protective space for her to be. My sense of the group during this time was that all group members had transformed themselves into willing selfobjects for Crystal. For her part, Crystal made it quite clear to the group that she felt extremely vulnerable and that she wished to be alone, to hide, and to remain mute.

After several more weeks had passed, the entire group began to join the vigil circle around her. When the entire group joined the circle, the mood of the group shifted. It became clear to all present that we were willing participants in a ritual that bore some semblance to a wake. We had become transformed into mourners at "a wake for a dead loved one." Indeed, we found ourselves mourning the loss of the Crystal that we had all known previously—the lively, gentle person that she had been prior to her brutal rape.

Then one day, Crystal began to peek out from under her blanket and she sat up. As she did so, her entire body, save her face, remained completely covered by her blanket. Several group members began to approach her, initially sitting diagonally across from her, and then gradually moving closer to her, and finally facing her frontally. As she began to make direct eye contact with those who looked directly at her, Crystal finally broke her silence by communicating with them through tapping sounds that she made with her fingers upon the wooden floor. At first, she tapped a variety of rhythms that were picked up by others and were emulated by them. Then, some group members began to introduce their own rhythms, to which she replied in kind. When several group members began to make sounds to accompany the tapping sounds they were making on different parts of their bodies, she followed suit. When she did so, it seemed as though Crystal was simultaneously liberating her body from the protective womb that had been provided by her security blanket. Once she moved away from her blanket, she began to move into the larger space around her in an investigatory and explorative way, while still continuing to tap various rhythms upon different parts of her body. As she tapped various parts of her body, she appeared to be awakening her body's vitality. Her physical resurrection had begun.

Following this period, Crystal's mood began to shift radically as she became engaged in creating some Ninja-like movements that she seemed to be directing toward some imaginary adversary. Other group members seemed eager to follow Crystal's lead, and they, too, began to battle imaginary foes. Then group members began to confront one another. When they did so, they introduced some humor into their encounters. They became engaged in what appeared to be mock "fight-flight" interactions with one another, which at times took on a playful and humorous tone. The intense, focused rage that Crystal had initially introduced into the group now began to subside under the influence of the group's lighter and more humorous touch. The raw rage initially introduced by Crystal was gradually transformed by the group into mocked forms of pretend fighting.

Then, one day, Crystal finally broke her silence. She spoke and reported that her assailant's case was coming up and that she would have to appear in court because she was the primary witness in the case. Several group members volunteered to drive her and to be present while the court proceedings were in session.

She expressed relief when the case was successfully concluded and her assailant was found guilty and incarcerated for a long time. When Crystal felt certain that her assailant would not be able to come after her, she began to talk openly about her experience with her husband, friends, and group members. As the group neared termination, space was given so that any group member who wished could "deal with something that had not yet been addressed by her." The group's cohesiveness and support for one another was palpable during these moments.

At the last group session, members had an opportunity to review what each had gotten from the group and to address those issues that remained unresolved for them. When it was Crystal's turn to speak, she addressed each group member individually and offered each a cutout square from her security blanket. Apparently, in preparation for the last session, Crystal had decided that she was ready to give up her blanket's protection by electing to transform it into an "object of gratitude." As she gave each member of the group a square piece from her blanket, she thanked each one for having given her "the strength and courage to survive." We were all deeply moved. Group members seemed to be very proud of the fact that they had met the challenge of being healing agents for a deeply wounded peer and had proven themselves equal to the task. For many group members, their participation in this healing process became their initiation into the field of dance/movement therapy.

RECLAIMING "SHADOW" PROJECTIONS AND FORGING AN AUTHENTIC SELF

Within the intimate sphere of psychosocial relationships that we forge with significant others is where we learn to emulate those personal qualities or actions that we admire, as well as emulate or resist those qualities that we dislike. When we leave our parental home, the public sphere of social relationships is where we learn to mediate the multiple identifications we forge with the various cultural groups to which we belong (Taylor, 1994). The sum of positive and negative identifications we form with others during our lifetime may be experienced as internal subjective splits. Although we find it easy to acknowledge positive identifications that we forge with others, we tend to project onto others, whom we dislike or fear, those negative qualities and behaviors that we feel ambivalent about or dislike in ourselves (see chapter 2 for a discussion on the process of "enemy-making").

ENACTING AND HEALING INTERNAL PARENTAL SPLITS

Helen is a 30-year-old woman with whom I worked privately through dance/movement therapy. Although she functioned well in the outside world, there were times when she would act in some self-destructive way with her family at home that reminded her of her own parents' destructive actions, an awareness that appalled her. However, she found it difficult to consciously acknowledge that she was in any way like her own parents, so that, whenever she would find herself acting like them, she would be surprised and deeply disappointed with herself and blame others for her behavior. A troubling dream she recounted in one of her sessions led her to a deeper understanding of how these negative split-off aspects of her own self-experience were in fact a legacy handed down to her by her parents (Dosamantes-Beaudry, 1999). She dreamed that a large ship that was heavily laden with cargo had become stranded at sea and had lost its bearings.

In dance/movement therapy, clients have an opportunity to identify through movement with objects and symbols that appear in their dreams and fantasies that carry a strong emotional charge for them. The following session describes how Helen became aware that the dreaded qualities she despised in her parents were also qualities that she herself possessed.

When Helen embodied the qualities she associated with "the lost ship" of her dream, she began to move aimlessly in many directions through space. She repeatedly lunged in one direction, followed by another. She repeated this movement pattern many times. When she stopped moving, she explained that she felt "totally lost" and that she experienced herself as having "no center." Her movements reminded her of her father, whom she characterized as being "irresponsible" and "untrustworthy." She contrasted his character with that of her mother, whom she viewed as "very responsible, very angry, and an extremely burdened person."

When she moved again, this time she moved as "the burdened ship" of her dreams. Her movement became slow and heavy. As she moved, not only did she experience "feeling burdened," but she also experienced being a "burdensome person" who felt "very resentful." When Helen finished moving, she recounted

how her parents had divorced because her parents "could not possibly live together any more."

When Helen resumed moving again, she returned to the dream of "the lost ship"
again. This time she found that, if she allowed herself to move freely and spontaneously as the "directionless ship," she was able to experience pleasure and joy
without having to have any other objective. By relinquishing control and by giving
herself over to the experience, Helen was able to discover her own spontaneity
and liveliness.

From a cognitive perspective, this session demonstrates how the spontaneity induced by the pretend playing that goes on in a dance/movement
therapy session enabled Helen to play with the movement metaphors that
she had created about her past self-experience. By moving or playing with
these metaphors in novel ways, the meaning that they previously held for
her shifted, giving rise to new perceptions and to the possibility of creating
a fresh new narrative about herself.

From a psychodynamic point of view, the embodiment of shadow or
split-off aspects of her self-experience, which previously were perceived
by Helen only in negative terms and not as a part of herself, shifted when
she was able to reclaim these negative identifications as her own in the
present. She also learned that if she "unburdened" herself from the notion
that she actually could control and be responsible for everything, she was
able to find joy and pleasure in her own spontaneity.

HEALING CULTURAL SPLITS AND FORGING AN
AUTHENTIC SELF

Members of racial or ethnic minorities who live in this country face the
dilemma of living between two worlds—the first defined by the norms
set by the dominant cultural group, and the second defined by the norms
set by members of their own racial or ethnic groups who carry the negative projections and lower social status granted them by the majority
cultural group. Being forced to carry the arbitrary and unwarranted projections of others undermines a recipient's sense of self in major ways that
do damage to his or her self-esteem.

Creative arts therapists are able to create a potential space where persons who carry the stigmatized projections of others may explore the
meaning that such stigmatized cultural identities hold for them and find
some ways to offset the negative effects that others' projections have upon
their self-integrity and self-worth. It has been my experience that clients
who possess dual hybrid or multicultural identities (in which one of their
cultural identities is devalued by a dominant cultural group) appreciate
a therapist who is able to acknowledge and show sensitivity about their
experience of living "between two worlds," makes an effort to become

better acquainted with their cultural worldview, and shows respect for their cultural traditions. What creative arts therapists can offer to persons who hold one or more stigmatized cultural identities is the opportunity to bridge the many dualities or experiential splits their clients have internalized as a result of being forced to carry others' unwarranted negative projections.

Irene was a dancer who was raised by parents who had emigrated from Central America to the United States before her birth. From birth onward, her parents had been interested in "having Irene take full advantage of all of the opportunities that this country could offer." For her this phrase came to mean that she should hide her Latina identity, not speak Spanish outside of her home, and do all that she could "to fit in" with the Anglo norms set by her teachers in school. At school, English was the only language found to be acceptable, and Anglo children seemed to be favored by her teachers.

Early in life, Irene showed talent as a dancer, so that she was able to obtain several scholarships to pursue her study of ballet. As she reached adolescence, she became a technically proficient ballet performer and was considered to be good enough to be hired by a well-known ballet company. The only problem she faced was that although she had become a brilliant technician, her own self-experience as a dancer was that of "a robot going through the motions." This view of herself was shared by the dance critics who had reviewed her solo performances. In their reviews of her dancing they commented that she possessed "great physical beauty" and was a "technical virtuoso" but they also noted that her performances "lacked fire" and that she seemed "to be detached" when she danced.

When I first met with her, she appeared to be not only very detached but also extremely depressed. During her first session, she mentioned that she had elected to seek dance therapy because "recently (she) had contemplated suicidal thoughts and fantasies, and dance was the one language through which she could communicate her experience well." She also shared some facts about her personal history, including her desire to fulfill her parents' dreams for her.

When she stopped talking, I suggested that she might wish to begin moving by "exploring the space within the studio in her own way, at her own pace." She smiled and automatically exhibited what I refer to as "a performer's persona." She began to execute a perfect series of balletic leaps and turns. Her ballet technique was superb. When she stopped moving, she waited for my reaction and to tell her what to do next. My sense was that she needed me to be there for her in two capacities: as a "mirroring self-object" to admire her, and as "a spark" to ignite her own sense of agency. I asked her what *she* would like to do next. She replied that she would like to move as though there were "no audience out there" (pointing toward me). I asked if she could imagine "a place where she could simply be without having an audience around to observe her and to judge her." She responded that "such a place existed only in [her] mind." Then she quickly changed her mind, and said that there was one place and that was in her own room. While in her own room, she "felt like herself" because, while there, she "could close the door." I suggested that she "imagine being in her own room, close the door, and move in whatever way she felt like."

She instantly curled up in one corner of the studio space and stayed curled up for a long time. In time, she gradually uncurled herself and attempted to stand up, her balance tentative and uncertain. Then suddenly she began to sob uncontrollably, plaintively crying out that she "felt like a newborn baby. I do not know who I am and I do not know how to move as me."

In the therapeutic work that followed, Irene proceeded to get in touch with her passivity and lack of autonomy as well as the anger she felt toward herself for having allowed herself to be molded into an automaton that bore some semblance of someone else's stereotyped notion of what it was "to be an American," which she felt to be a false facade that did not accurately reflect who she actually felt herself to be. As she increasingly began to move on her own initiative, in a self-directed way, those qualities that she had hidden from others and from herself, for fear of not being in keeping with the false American image that she was attempting to fulfill, began to surface.

Initially in her search for her true identity, her movement patterns took on the qualities possessed by wild animals whose motions are entirely driven by their own impulses. Over time, the various forms her movements assumed took on a variety of animal forms. At first she was "a light fragile butterfly," then she became "a powerful, earthbound tigress," and finally she was transformed into a more "feeling human ballerina." Also, as she began "to move from (her) heart," she was able to reveal her passion, or "fire," that she had hidden so well from herself and others. By allowing herself to move spontaneously in a self-directed way that followed her own internal impulses of the moment to be expressed, Irene gradually became better acquainted with a self that she experienced as being "more authentic." Winnicott (1965) has referred to a person's experience of authenticity as a person's "True Self" (p. 142).

Winnicott (1965) noted that when primary caregivers consistently ignore their child's needs and instead demand their child's compliance to their own standards, needs, and wishes, the child soon learns to adopt a "False Self" (p. 142). According to him, the False Self is a coping strategy that children adopt to "hide and protect the True Self" (Winnicott, 1965, p. 142). However, the cost to the child for adopting a False Self is that she or he feels unreal and lives with a profound sense of emptiness and futility. A True Self feels "real" to the child. Its existence is best reflected in the child's capacity to create a "spontaneous gesture" (Winnicott, 1965, p. 140):

The True Self comes from the aliveness of the body tissues and the working of body-functions, including the heart's action and breathing (Winnicott, 1965, p. 148).

SUMMARY OF CASE VIGNETTES

This chapter has provided several examples of the work of creative arts therapists with clients who functioned at different levels of self-other differentiation and regressive states, and who needed to reorganize their self-experience and self-structure to adequately negotiate a difficult developmental transition they were confronting, or, in the case of Crystal, to cope with a temporary, structural regression that was set into motion by a sudden cataclysmic event.

The clients of art therapist Jean Davis (1999) and drama therapists Craig Haen and Kenneth Brannon (2002) presented in this chapter all had personal histories that included extreme emotional deprivation, abuse, and abandonment. The deleterious effects produced by such a derailed development upon a person's sense of self and emotional functioning are immeasurable.

Davis's (1999) community park project traced the path of destruction, reconfiguration, and reconstruction that one homeless shelter resident underwent as she became invested in creating her own sculpture for the shelter's community park. The outward process involved in creating her sculpture paralleled the shifts that her internal self-experience underwent, as she gradually began to create a more coherent sense of herself.

The roles of superhero, monster, and baby preferred by the latency-aged boys who participated in Haen and Brannon's (2002) drama therapy groups provided these boys with an opportunity to engage in pretend play and to enact the psychodynamic and symbolic meaning that such fantasied characters held for them through role playing. This role-playing process allowed the boys to internalize alternative, more age-appropriate strategies to get their emotional needs met.

Children and adults who face serious life-threatening illnesses often experience multiple losses (loss of social power and self-control, loss of self-esteem, loss of body-image constancy, and loss of social relationships). A healing art-making process offers seriously ill persons an opportunity to forge a safe relationship with an intermediary, playful art medium that can be directed and regulated by them, and through which they can begin to express their unspeakable thoughts and emotions, and ultimately acquire some sense of mastery over the difficult circumstances they face (Fenton, 2000; Gunter, 2000).

Children who suffer from repeated traumas that have been inflicted by adults upon whom they must rely for their survival and emotional support face the paradoxical challenge of being terrified of the very people upon whom they must depend for their safety and support. Infants who have experienced repeated traumas at the hands of their caregivers frequently have no verbal recollection that such an emotionally disruptive event has taken place. Sometimes the only recall they have as adults that such an event has actually occurred is through the manifestation of some kind of somatic symptom. The case of Emily illustrates how her "pain-rage dance" helped her recall the repeated invasions to her body space that she had experienced as an infant at the hands of her mother. Being able to recall a traumatic missing piece from her early past allowed Emily to synthesize the meaning that this experience held for her in the present.

The regressive impact that a sudden, unexpected, situational threatening event can have upon a victim was demonstrated by Crystal, a participant in a long-term dance/movement therapy group. The unconditional support that she received from her dance/movement therapy group allowed her to enact and to synthesize the meaning that her rape and abduction held for her so that she could recover her emotional balance. When the group ended, Crystal was not the same person who had died emotionally on the day that her traumatic experience took place, but a person who possessed a stronger and clearer sense of herself.

The cases of Helen and Irene illustrate how previously denied and despised shadow aspects of their self-experience, which were part of the legacy passed down by their parents or were projected to them by others as unwanted aspects of themselves, became detoxified and transformed by them into more benign forms of self-experience that they could reassimilate into their adult self-experience. By being able to reclaim disavowed aspects of their self-experience, Helen and Irene's emotional tolerance and compassion for themselves and others grew.

Chapter 5 describes the public sphere of social relationships as the site where various forms of cultural artistic expressions are created, and where, in turn, the social positions adopted by members of various cultural groups are mediated through the manipulation of cultural art symbols.

NOTE

1. As used here, the term object constancy refers to one's acquisition of cognitive object permanence as well as the capacity to contain one's ambivalent emotional reactions toward others.

REFERENCES

Azar, B. (2002, March). The power of pretending. *Monitor on Psychology, 33* (3), 46–48.

Betsy, A. (1997). *Icons: Magnets of meaning*. San Francisco: Chronicle Books.

Borgmann, E. (2002). Art therapy with three women diagnosed with cancer. *Arts in Psychotherapy Journal, 29* (4), 245–251.

Bowlby, J. M. (1984). Clinical applications of theories of attachment and loss. Introductory remarks and case consultation. *Seminars on tape* [Cassette recording]. Los Angeles: Lifespan Learning Institute.

Davis, J. (1999). Report: Environmental art therapy-metaphors in the field. *Arts in Psychotherapy Journal, 26* (1), 45–49.

Dosamantes-Alperson, E. (1979). The intrapsychic and the interpersonal in experiential movement psychotherapy. *American Journal of Dance Therapy, 3,* 20–31.

Dosamantes-Alperson, E. (1985). A current perspective of imagery in psychoanalysis. *Imagination, Cognition and Personality, 15* (3), 199–209.

Dosamantes-Beaudry, I. (1997a). Embodying a cultural identity. *Arts in Psychotherapy Journal, 24* (2), 129–135.

Dosamantes-Beaudry, I. (1997b). Somatic experience in psychoanalysis. *Psychoanalytic Psychology, 14* (4), 517–530.

Dosamantes-Beaudry, I. (1999). A psychoanalytically-informed application of dance/movement therapy. In D. J. Wiener (Ed.), *Beyond talk therapy* (pp. 245–262). Washington, DC: American Psychological Association.

Dosamantes-Beaudry, I. (2001). Frida Kahlo: Self-other representation and self healing through art. *Arts in Psychotherapy Journal, 28* (1), 5–17.

Dosamantes-Beaudry, I. (2002). Frida Kahlo: The creation of a cultural icon. *Arts in Psychotherapy Journal, 29* (1), 3–12.

Edinger, E. F. (1992). *Ego and archetype.* Boston: Shambala Publications.

Erikson, E. H. (1968). *Identity: Youth and crisis* (2nd ed.). New York: Norton.

Estes, P. C. (1995). *Women who run with the wolves.* New York: Ballantine Books.

Fenton, J. F. (2000). Cystic fibrosis in art therapy. *Arts in Psychotherapy Journal, 27* (1), 15–25.

Freud, S. (1958). Formulation on the two principles of mental functioning. In *The standard edition of the complete psychological works of Sigmund Freud* (Vol. 12, pp. 218–226). London: Hogarth Press. (Original work published 1911.)

Gunter, M. (2000). Art therapy as an intervention to stabilize the defense of children undergoing bone marrow transplantation. *Arts in Psychotherapy Journal, 27* (1), 3–14.

Haen, C., & Brannon, K. H. (2002). Superheroes, monsters and babies: Roles of strength, destruction and vulnerability for emotionally disturbed boys. *Arts in Psychotherapy Journal, 29* (1), 31–40.

Hedges, L. E. (1983). *Listening perspectives in psychology.* New York: Jason Aronson.

Jung, C. G. (1964). *Man and his symbols.* New York: Bantam Doubleday Dell Publishing Group.

Jung, C. G. (1976). Symbols and the interpretation of dreams. *Collected Works* (Vol. 18, pp. 185–266). Princeton, NJ: Princeton University Press. (Original work published 1961.)

Kernberg, O. (1976). *Object relations theory and clinical psychoanalysis.* New York: Jason Aronson.

Klein, M. (1975). *Envy and gratitude and other works 1946–1963.* New York: The Free Press.

Knafo, D. (2002). Revisiting Kris's concept of regression in the service of the ego in art. *Psychoanalytic Psychology, 19* (1), 24–29.

Kohut, H. (1984). *How does analysis cure?* Chicago: University of Chicago Press.

Kris, E. (1952). *Psychoanalytic explorations in art.* New York: International Universities Press.

Krueger, D. W. (1989). *Body self and psychological self.* New York: Brunner/ Mazel Publishers.

Kubler-Ross, E. (1969). *On death and dying.* New York: Macmillan.

Landy, R. J. (1994). *Drama therapy: Concepts, theories and practices* (2nd ed.). Springfield, IL: Charles C. Thomas.

Mahler, M., Pine, I., & Bergman, A. (1975). *The psychological birth of the human infant.* New York: Basic Books.

Main, M. (1999). Epilogue: Attachment theory: Eighteen points with suggestions for future studies. In J. Cassidy & P. R. Shaver (Eds.), *Handbook of attachment: Theory, research and clinical applications* (pp. 845–888). New York: Guildford Press.

McDougall, J. (1989). *Theatres of the body: A psychoanalytic approach to psychosomatic illness.* London: Free Association Books.

Neborsky, R. (2002). Introduction in *Attachment: From early childhood through the lifespan* (pp. 1–4). Los Angeles: UCLA Extension and Lifespan Learning Institute.

Orange, D. (1992). Subjectivism, relativism, and realism in psychoanalysis. In A. Goldberg (Ed.), *New therapeutic visions: Progress in self psychology: Vol. 8* (pp. 189–197). Hillsdale, NJ: Analytic Press.

Piaget, J. (1967). *Six psychological studies.* New York: Vintage Books.

Raphael-Leff, J. (1994). Imaginative bodies of childrearing: Visions and revisions. In *The imaginative body* (pp. 13–42). Northvale, NJ: Aronson.

Schuster, C. S., & Ashburn, S. S. (1992). *The process of human development: A holistic life-span approach.* Philadelphia: Lippincott.

Siegel, D. J. (2001). Memory: An overview, with emphasis on developmental, interpersonal and neurobiological aspects. *Journal of American Academy of Child Adolescent Psychiatry, 40* (9), 997–1011.

Squire, L. R. (1987). *Memory and brain.* New York: Oxford University Press.

Stolorow, R. D., Brandchaft, B., & Atwood, G. (1987). *Psychoanalytic treatment: An intersubjective approach.* Hillsdale, NJ: The Analytic Press.

Stolorow, R. D., & Lachman, F. (1980). *Psychoanalysis of developmental arrests.* New York: International Universities Press.

Taylor, C. (1994). The politics of recognition. In D. T. Goldberg (Ed.), *Multiculturalism: A critical reader* (pp. 75–106). Malden, MA: Blackwell.

Winnicott, D. W. (1965). *The maturational processes of the facilitating environment.* New York: International Universities Press.

Winnicott, D. W. (1982). *Playing and reality.* New York: Penguin Books.

CHAPTER 5

The Public Social Sphere: Site of Artistic Cultural Expression and Communal Healing

CULTURAL WORLDVIEW AND EXPRESSIVE STYLE

The worldview of a particular culture is revealed through the expressive styles and aesthetic choices its members make. Cultural worldviews gain much of their power by virtue of being implicitly or unconsciously transacted through nonverbal modes of expression (Hall, 1966). For example, members of different cultures tend to establish different kinds of interpersonal distances across various kinds of social contexts.

One can study cultural aesthetic differences by studying the structural differences that exist in the art forms that are favored by different cultural groups. For instance, Japanese traditional dances reflect the traditional and collectivist worldview values of traditional Japanese society. In these dances, the dancer does not seek to stand out. The ideal way of moving is to move without appearing to move, to glide through space without lifting the back of the foot or heel from the ground. Virtuosity is displayed through restraint and subtlety (Masakato & Cohen, 1983). In contrast, contemporary classical ballet valorizes the modernist and individualist worldview of contemporary Western societies. This form of dance emphasizes the athletic prowess of the individual performer, the dancer's capacity to cover a wide expanse of space, and the air-bound movements that give the impression of transcending gravity.

As adults we learn what the arts symbolize and mean to us from the way we personally experience them in our lives and through the way our cultural institutions define the arts and treat art makers. In everyday life, we make use of symbols, including art symbols, to negotiate our various social positions of status and power, which we enact within the public social sphere of human relationships.

In sum, what we find to be aesthetically pleasing, emotionally gratifying, and appropriate to express is shaped and determined by the worldviews of the people of the society in which we live. One's cultural worldview provides a framework and an orientation for the ways that one should feel, think, and function in the world. It does this by providing a context of dynamic symbols and meanings that we repeatedly create and re-create for ourselves while in the process of interacting socially with others (Geertz, 1973). Our cultural worldview acts as a filter for what we pay attention to and what we ignore. It encompasses shared values, myths, attitudes, and behavioral norms that influence the way we make sense of the world in which we live; the feelings we express or inhibit; the subjective sense of self we construct; the attitudes we form about ourselves, others, and the world; and what we consider to be appropriate norms of comportment (Dosamantes-Beaudry, 1999; Markus & Kitayama, 1991).

The latent aspects of culture are effective because they function silently and unconsciously. They are most readily revealed by the way members of a given society move in space, the rhythms they generate while interacting with others, the way its people dress and decorate themselves and their environment, the objects they create, and the way they express themselves linguistically, particularly through the metaphors and idioms that they use. Collectively, this expressive behavioral repertoire gives a particular culture its own distinctive style. An examination of a culture's expressive style reveals less conscious, more stable aspects of a people's collective worldview (Dosamantes, 1992). For example, the Western American idiom, "the squeaky wheel gets the grease," reflects an individualist-modernist worldview and lifestyle orientation, whereas the Japanese idiom, "the nail that stands out gets pounded," reflects a collectivist-traditionalist worldview and lifestyle orientation, respectively (Markus & Kitayama, 1991).

How the arts are defined and the kinds of social roles that artists are permitted to play depends upon the collective worldview of the particular culture being sampled during a particular moment in time. In the West, for instance, during medieval times, artists were considered to be mere instruments of God through which His divine inspiration was conveyed. During the Renaissance, a paradigm shift occurred toward the human, causing artists to be perceived as individuals of genius, endowed with extraordinary gifts and original visions. The romantic movement of the nineteenth century cast artists into the roles of social outcasts and rebels from society and as individuals who were willing to sacrifice everything for their art (Apostolos-Cappadona & Ebersole, 1997).

What the arts mean to the various constituencies of a society at any given moment in time is always being negotiated within the public sphere of psychosocial relationships that they establish. For instance, during the 1960s, artists who became affiliated with various civil rights movements of this country were critical of Western art mythologies fashioned after and for the sole benefit of the white male of the species. During this time, artists who identified with a feminist political agenda became publicly critical of being denied equal access to educational opportunities, public performance venues, and gallery spaces because of their gender (Apostolos-Cappadona & Ebersole, 1997).

Dissatisfied with the marginalized status granted them by the dominant culture, these politicized artists began to press for equal educational and work opportunities. Many chose to define themselves through their art, and to depict in their artwork the kinds of social injustices they had experienced in their lives (Braude & Garrard, 1996). They introduced into their artwork the notion that gender, race, and ethnic identities are socially constructed concepts. They challenged the view of "high" versus "low" art and the myth of the "artist as genius" being promoted by the Western art establishment. In their artwork, these artists chose not to privilege any one artistic style, but instead elected to support a wide variety of multi-cultural artistic styles (Braude & Garrard; Gaspar de Alba, 1998; Ybarra-Frausto, 1992). The artwork of Los Angeles artist and chair of the Art Department at UCLA, Barbara Drucker, for example, represents the "alternative" voice of a Western contemporary woman artist. In an interview I conducted with her about her artwork, she described her experience during her formative years as an art student (Drucker, 2002).

She recounted that, while in college, she had been discouraged by her male professors from representing her personal experience through her artwork. She had been told that "Art was about form and not content" and "that what mattered in Art was the universal and not the personal."

As a mature artist, her artwork provides evidence of the shift in social consciousness that has resulted from the initiatives that were introduced by feminist women artists during the 1960s. Commenting upon gender differences, she stated that "men's artwork differs from women's" but that she "felt comfortable drawing upon (her) own personal experiences to create art." While preparing an installation, *Material Evidence*, exhibited by the Fine Arts Council of the University of Judaism in February, 2002, she drew upon the metaphor of "making art from familiar found objects" as inspiration for the work (see Photo 5.1). This artwork is a vibrant, colorful construction made of braided wool that is partially woven and partially unraveled. To the artist, her artwork "is a work in progress, representing the mid-point of a woman's life." It is not only intended "to honor woman's traditional work as a weaver of relationships" but also to reflect the deeper "symbolic and psychological meaning of woman's daily work-as life-giver, nurturer and builder."

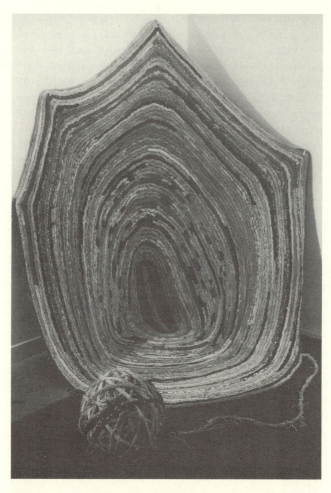

Photo 5.1   *Material Evidence: Braided Rug with Ball* by Barbara
Drucker. Mixed media exhibit, *Material Concerns: Poetry in
Space,* The Fine Arts Council of the University of Judaism,
Los Angeles, February 10–April 4, 2000.

The interactive social relationships that evolve between groups holding
different or opposing social positions and interests is best exemplified
through the evolving psychosocial relationships that they create with one
another and through the way they make use of the objects and artistic
symbols that they create to valorize their social positions. These evolving
public relationships not only reflect the socioeconomic conditions and resources available to a society at a given moment in time, but also reflect

the social status, political views, aesthetic values, and psychodynamic needs and motives of the constituent cultural groups of a society.

How the social agendas of various groups that are in conflict with one another get played out in their everyday interactions with one another is illustrated by Moreno (1999). He has described the psychosocial relationships that unfolded between two different cultural groups, World War II concentration camp inmates, who happened to be musicians wishing to survive their ordeal, and concentration camp officials, who hated Jews and other ethnic groups but were interested in forming concentration camp orchestras with musicians drawn from the inmate population.

For those musicians who were either gifted enough or lucky enough to be auditioned and to be selected for the camp orchestras, playing a musical instrument became a palpable means of holding on to life and also a means of temporarily transcending the terrifying conditions that otherwise filled their lives. Less fortunate inmates who where were scheduled to die in the camp's gas chambers were often escorted to their deaths as camp musicians played on. Ostensibly, this was done to reduce the doomed inmates' terror, but also, for the Nazi camp officials, this act seemed to blot out any sense of responsibility they might assume for the atrocities that they were committing. Camp officials often requested that camp orchestras play their favorite pieces of music to conjure up more pleasant memories of happier times and events in their lives. The use of music under such extreme and dire circumstances, in which one group holds the power of life and death over another, underscores how the arts can be used and manipulated by different cultural groups to support their life-preserving as well as their life-destroying impulses, intentions, and actions.

CULTURAL WORLDVIEW AND THE APPROPRIATENESS AND EFFECTIVENESS OF CULTURE-SPECIFIC HEALING PRACTICES

Two experiences that all living human beings share in common during their lifetime are the leaving of old familiar worlds and the reentry into new unknown worlds (Golan, 1981). *Transitions* are processes that allow one to negotiate the difficult kinds of changes that one encounters while in the process of leaving and returning. This book addresses two kinds of transitions that individuals and groups in crisis can negotiate through the use of art-making as a healing process. The first is the developmental transition, generally associated with life cycle changes, in which changes are expected and often occur gradually. The second is the external transition, which is set into motion by unexpected catastrophic events that often occur suddenly and without warning. Both of these kinds of transitions encompass three phases: (a) phase one begins when one lets go of the ways things have been, (b) phase two is an in-between state that is often experienced as chaotic or disquieting and sets in motion some degree of regression that offers one the potential to acquire a fresh perspective, and (c) phase three occurs when one comes to terms with the way things have actually become and reconnects with the world one has left behind (Bridges, 2001; Turner, 1987, Van Gennep, 1960).

Traditional cultures long ago acknowledged the fact that critical life cycle changes occur to everyone during their lives. They, therefore, created structures in the form of rites of passage to regulate those developmental transitions that they acknowledged as a society. Most traditional cultures recognize the developmental transitions that are involved in being born, coming of age, marrying, having a child, joining the circle of elders, and dying (Van Gennep, 1960).

According to Turner (1969, 1987), rites of passage can be found in all societies, but they tend to reach maximal expression in small-scale, homogeneous, relatively stable societies whose observance of change is tied to cyclical changes in nature. Examples of such rituals may be found among contemporary Native American tribal communities. For instance, in the ritual of the Cheyenne Vision Quest, a boy is prepared for months by an older male to undergo the ordeal of living alone for four days and nights without water or food in the sacred mountain. Through the successful negotiation of this ordeal, the boy's status in the community is transformed to that of a man. On a mythical level, this ritual is a story about a hero who leaves behind childhood and goes off alone to seek vision, insight, and meaning (Madhi, Foster, & Little, 1987). In the Mescalero Apache White Painted Woman's ritual, a girl is transformed into a woman while symbolically reenacting the four stages of an Apache woman's life and White Painted Woman's journey through the eons (Nagy, 1987). Native American communities have also created rituals that allow them to cope with external transitions. For example, the Navajo Enemy Way is a ritual that attempts to cleanse returning warriors from the deleterious effects of the trauma of war and helps them readjust to a peacetime society (Manson et al., 1996).

We can admire and learn much from the cultural traditions and rituals that are practiced by cultural groups whose worldviews differ from our own. However, as outsiders, we cannot simply appropriate other people's customs and practices and put them on like overcoats. Csikszentmihalyi (1990) offers an explanation for why this is the case:

The wisdom of the mystics, of the Sufi, of the great yogis, or the Zen masters might have been excellent in their own time and might still be best, if we lived in those times and in those cultures. But transplanted to contemporary California, those systems lose quite a bit of their original power . . . (because) they contain elements that are specific to their original contexts (p. 21).

The strategies and practices we adopt to modify our consciousness, to discover meaningful life goals, and to find effective coping strategies for meeting life's challenges, are all culture specific. Furthermore, one's cultural worldview also influences the meaning and subjective experience of trauma in a differential way (Marsella, Friedman, Gerrity, & Scurfield, 1996). What might be considered to be a rite of passage in one cultural setting may be regarded as a traumatic event in another.

Ramirez and Castaneda (1974) have suggested that cultural beliefs, values, and styles can be classified along a traditionalist to modernist dimension. According to these authors, a traditional orientation to life appears to be prevalent among rural communities, conservative religions, and "third world" societies. People who identify with traditional cultures tend to emphasize spiritual explanations for the mysteries of life and to be strongly identified with their families and communities of origin. Also, they are likely to believe in the separation of gender and age roles and to adopt autocratic approaches to child rearing.

In contrast, a modernist orientation to life is found primarily among urban communities, liberal religions, and dominant cultural groups of both the United States and Western Europe. People who identify with a modernist value system tend to resort to scientific explanations to comprehend the mysteries of life. They tend to hold a strong individualistic orientation and to de-emphasize differences in gender and age roles while stressing egalitarian child-rearing practices (Ramirez & Castaneda, 1974).

When studying the issues of cultural identity, a unidimensional view of race or ethnicity and discrete, dichotomous descriptors are no longer viable to describe the cultural complexities of our contemporary, multicultural American society. This is because today, many Americans hold several cultural ethnic identities at once, each composed of a dynamic network of attitudes and beliefs that may be concordant or discordant with one another (Goode, 1960). Therefore, sole dominant identifications are no longer adequate to represent the range of cultural diversity and cultural hybridity that exists in our contemporary society (Gusman et al., 1996). For instance, recently when golf professional Tiger Woods was asked by a news media reporter how he would characterize his ethnicity, he responded that he refers to himself as "Cablinasian" because this term encompasses all of the ethnic roots of his ethnic ancestry—a mixture of Caucasian, Black, American Indian, and Asian (Sokolove, 2002, p. 35). Anticipating the inevitable increase in ethnic and racial hybridity that will result in the future, Vasconcelos (1961) envisioned the emergence of a fifth race in the future. Such a race would embrace the four major races that are presently recognized within contemporary, culturally heterogeneous societies. Anzaldua (1997) posits that such a hybrid race would have the

potential to enrich the human gene pool by giving rise to a "mestiza consciousness" that could better tolerate conflict and ambiguity (p. 233).

Culturally heterogeneous societies stand to benefit greatly from the
broad range of talents represented by the diverse cultural groups residing
in them. However, they are also more likely to be vulnerable to the social
conflict that results when constituent diverse cultural groups do not get
along with one another and decide to mediate their grievances through
violence. Heterogeneous societies face the difficult task of finding peaceful
accommodations to the differences that exist among their diverse constituent cultural groups, marked by differences in language, gender, race,
ethnicity, religion, economic class, geography, customs, and rituals. One
problem that culturally heterogenous societies confront during times of
crisis is not having a commonly shared way of observing transitions.

The punishment of American diversity is that we are denied the warmth of shared
ritual. We have no common text for bereavement, no outstretched hand from the
ancient world upon which to rely as a truly single culture. We've been winging
it, secret sharers who cobble our rituals from a very recent history (Sella, 2001,
p. 48).

Also because the religious, educational, and health care systems that
exist to support us during times of crisis function independently of one
another, many of us find it difficult to cope in a coherent way with the
developmental and external life transitions that cause us great anxiety.
And so we do so privately and alone. As a result, we are deprived of the
depth of meaning, self-integration, and social relatedness than we might
otherwise obtain, if we were able to negotiate such transitions within the
context of a shared group ritual. Scheff (1979) has referred to this state of
affairs as the "deritualization" of Western societies (p. 128). He contends
that culturally sanctioned rituals perform a vital function for individuals
by allowing them to set the right emotional distance to an unbearable
situation.

Our cultural worldview not only influences our sense of reality, and our
sense of who we are, but it also influences the way we construe healing
and the practices we turn to for healing. Schmais (1998) has pointed out
some important differences that exist between shaman and medicine
women and men who come from homogeneous tribal societies that follow
oral traditions and Western health care practitioners who lead modernist
lifestyles and live in high-tech, culturally heterogeneous, literate societies.
The former have their cultural roots in polytheistic, animistic mythologies,
and their spiritual, educational, and social spheres of life tend to be integrated functionally and spatially. In contrast, contemporary Western health
care workers, including creative arts therapists, live in societies that are
rooted in monotheism and scientific empiricism. The primary social unit

of these cultures is the nuclear family, in which individuals operate functionally within discrete social spheres. In these societies, religious, educational, and health care systems function independently of one another. The role of the healer is acquired through formal training provided by secular educational institutions.

During contemporary times, those of us who lead Western modernist lifestyles in a society that has compartmentalized and institutionalized so many critical aspects of living are often ill prepared to deal with the emotional disruption that extreme catastrophic and developmental changes generate. When confronting great emotional pain, we fear losing control and being overwhelmed by chaos. As a society that prizes autonomy and individuality greatly, we learn to suffer in silence, alone. Our dread of emotional pain and emotional disruption is shared and reinforced by the predominant Western medical model, which views intense emotional disruption as something negative and symptomatic of an underlying pathological process that must be promptly circumvented and suppressed through the use of psychopharmacological drugs. This phobic view of emotional pain and emotional disruption becomes magnified when we attempt to negotiate any of the phases involved in a transition process, making the negotiation of any critical life transition even more difficult.

SOCIAL ISOLATION:
AILMENT OF CONTEMPORARY SOCIETIES

In a society that values independence, individuality, competitiveness, mobility, and material possessions as much as ours does, it is not surprising that as we mature, we experience considerable loneliness and isolation (Almond, 1974; Slater, 1970). Almond compared the social position occupied by twentieth-century Western man to his nineteenth-century predecessor by noting:

[Twentieth-century man] is richer, more socially and geographically mobile, better able to choose from a variety of external experiences in his leisure. But he lacks the inner experience of meaning, interconnectedness and stable social position of his more limited predecessor (p. 229).

In 1969, Turner observed that a central function of the healing ceremonies practiced by tribal societies was the temporary undoing of all distinctions among community members based on role and social status differences. He coined the term "communitas" to refer to a group of people for whom the usual distinction among members based on such differences gave way to a more basic relatedness, and group members were free to confront one another openly and without fear of retribution (Turner, 1969, p. 177).

During the 1960s in this country, several kinds of groups were formed with the intention of creating communities that encouraged relationships among social equals and in which open communication between group members was encouraged. Some of the groups that were formed during this time were time limited in nature and lasted from several days to several months (e.g., encounter groups). Other groups evolved into more lasting communities (e.g., Synanon and some self-help communes).

The encounter group phenomenon of the 1960s was a diffuse social movement that touched a wide spectrum of American life. It attracted people from the hippie counterculture and radical political movements as well as millions of "straight" middle- and upper-middle-class Americans who were searching for greater personal meaning and more meaningful social relatedness (Almond, 1974). Slater (1970) has suggested that the popularity of encounter groups was due in large part to our need for a sense of *communitas* and for increased engagement and dependence upon one another (p. 5). In encounter groups, members learned to listen to one another in nonjudgmental ways and to provide support for one another. They acquired a deeper understanding of one another by developing the ability to understand and to tolerate each other's point of view (Rogers, 1970).

Rogers (1970) has noted that all effective encounter groups move through similar group phases. In the beginning phase, individuals who are strangers to one another try to become acclimated to the group. They begin to identify group goals, to set rules, and to determine each member's reasons for joining the group. During the initial group phase, interactions between group members are often superficial. The first challenge for the group generally arises over issues of power and control. Different factions appear and the group becomes splintered into smaller subgroups. In these subgroups, members turn to each other for support and for protection against members of other subgroups, whom they perceive as outsiders. Conflict among group factions around issues of power and control becomes heightened during this time. As this conflict becomes resolved through dialogue, each person's involvement with and commitment to the whole group deepens.

During the middle phase of the group's process, members begin to increasingly trust one another. They become more disclosing about themselves, and intimacy within the group surfaces. As the sense of intimacy increases between group members, they begin to explore the issues they raise within the group in a deeper way. They begin to grant each other greater freedom of expression and they increasingly validate and accept the ideas and feelings of other group members. The group begins to develop a sense of cohesiveness. They show increased tolerance for differences of all kinds. Various ways of viewing and dealing with issues are recognized and acknowledged.

During the third and final phase of the group's process, the group faces the prospect of acknowledging the goals that have been met or have not been achieved by members. Group members also come to terms with the prospect of termination and separation. Generally, the phases followed by effective encounter groups seem to parallel the phases of the transition process outlined at the beginning of chapter 2.

Chapter 6 focuses on the group work of several gifted creative arts therapists and renowned artists who have made use of a group art-making healing process to restore the emotional balance of group members and to promote greater social relatedness and empathy among them.

REFERENCES

Almond, R. (1974). *The healing community.* New York: Jason Aronson.

Anzaldua, G. (1997). La conciencia de la mestiza. Towards a new consciousness. In K. Conboy, N. Medina, & S. Stanbury (Eds.), *Writing on the body* (pp. 233–247). New York: Columbia University Press.

Apostolos-Cappadona, D., & Ebersole, L. (1997). *Women, creativity and the arts.* New York: Continuum Publishing.

Braude, N., & Garrard, M. D. (1996). *The power of feminist art.* New York: Harry N. Abrams.

Bridges, W. (2001). *The way of transition: Embracing life's most difficult moments.* Cambridge, MA: Perseum Publishing.

Csikszentmihalyi, M. (1990). *Flow: The psychology of optimal experience.* New York: Harper & Row.

Dosamantes, I. (1992). Body-image. Repository for cultural idealizations and denigrations of the self. *Arts in Psychotherapy Journal, 19,* 257–267.

Dosamantes-Beaudry, I. (1999). Divergent cultural self construals: Implications for the practice of dance/movement therapy. *Arts in Psychotherapy Journal, 26* (4), 225–231.

Drucker, B. (2002, May 18). Personal Communication.

Gaspar de Alba, A. (1998). *Chicano art: Inside outside the master's house.* Austin, TX: University of Texas Press.

Geertz, C. (1973). *The interpretation of cultures.* New York: Basic Books.

Golan, N. (1981). *Passing through transitions.* New York: The Free Press.

Goode, W. J. (1960). A theory of role strain. *American Sociological Review, 25,* 483–496.

Gusman, F. D., Stewart, J., Hiley Young, B., Riney, S. J., Abueg, F. R., & Blake, D. D. (1996). A multicultural developmental approach to treating trauma. In A. J. Marsella, M. J. Friedman, E. T. Gerrity, & R. M. Scurfield (Eds.), *Ethnocultural aspects of posttraumatic stress disorders* (pp. 439–459). Washington, DC: American Psychological Association.

Hall, E. T. (1966). *The hidden dimension.* New York: Doubleday.

Madhi, L. C., Foster, S., & Little, M. (1987). *Betwixt & between: Patterns of masculine and feminine initiation.* LaSalle, IL: Open Court Publishing.

Manson, S., Beals, J., O'Neill, T., Piasecki, J., Bechtold, D., Keane, E., & Jones, M. (1996). Wounded spirits, ailing hearts: PTSD and related disorders, among American Indians. In A. J. Marsella, M. J. Friedman, E. T. Gerrity, & R. M. Scurfield (Eds.), *Ethnocultural aspects of posttaumatic stress disorder* (pp. 255–283). Washington, DC: American Psychological Association.

Markus, H. R., & Kitayama, S. (1991). Culture and the self: Implications for cognition, emotion and motivation. *American Psychologist, 98* (2), 224–253.

Marsella, S. J., Friedman, M. J., Gerrity, E. T., & Scurfield, R. M. (1996). *Ethnocultural aspects of posttraumatic stress disorder.* Washington, DC: American Psychological Association.

Masakato, G., & Cohen, S. J. (1983). Virtuosity and the aesthetic ideals of Japanese dance and virtuosity and the aesthetic ideals of Western classical dance. *Dance Research Annual, XIV,* 88–95.

Moreno, J. (1999). Orpheus in hell: Music and therapy in the holocaust. *Arts in Psychotherapy Journal, 26* (1), 3–14.

Nagy, M. (1987). Singing for life: The Mescalero Apache girl's puberty ceremony. In L. C. Madhi, S. Foster, & M. Little (Eds.), *Betwixt and between: Patterns of masculine and feminine initiation* (pp. 239–263). LaSalle, IL: Open Court.

Ramirez, M., & Castaneda, A. (1974). *Cultural democracy, bicognitive development and education.* New York: Academic Press.

Rogers, C. (1970). *On encounter groups.* New York: Harper & Row.

Scheff, T. J. (1979). *Catharsis in healing, ritual and drama.* Berkeley, CA: University of California Press.

Schmais, C. (1998). Creative arts therapies and shamanism. *Arts in Psychotherapy Journal, 15,* 281–284.

Sella, M. (2001, October 7). How a grief ritual is born. *The New York Times Magazine,* pp. 48–51.

Slater, P. (1970). *The pursuit of loneliness.* Boston: Beacon.

Sokolove, M. (2002, July 14). The Tiger Files. A taxonomy of a post-everything pop icon. *The New York Times Magazine,* pp. 32–36.

Turner, V. W. (1969). *The ritual process.* Chicago: Aldine.

Turner, V. W. (1987). Betwixt and between: The limenal period of rites of passage. In L. Carus Madhi, S. Foster, & M. Little (Eds.), *Bewixt and between: Patterns of masculine and feminine initiation* (pp. 3–19). LaSalle, IL: Open Court.

Van Gennep, A. (1960). *The rites of passage.* Chicago, IL: University of Chicago Press.

Vasconcelos, J. (1961). La raza cosmica: Mision de la raza Ibero-Americana. Mexico City: Aguilar S. A. de Ediciones.

Ybarra-Frausto, T. (1992). Rasquachismo: A Chicano sensibility. In R. Griswold Del Castillo, T. McKenna, & R. Yarbro-Bejarano (Eds.), *Chicano art, resistance and affirmation 1965–1985* (pp. 155–161). Los Angeles: Wight Art Gallery, UCLA.

CHAPTER 6

The Creation of *Communitas* through Group Art-Making

The public sphere of interpersonal relationships is where we construct the multiple cultural identities that we forge within the social groups to which we belong (Taylor, 1994). It is in the public sphere that we mediate our various cultural identities and generate the conflicts that exist among different cultural groups. During contemporary times, maintaining cordial relationships among diverse cultural groups has become a pressing concern for our culturally heterogeneous, high-tech society. This concern has become focused around several highly contested social issues that include the representation of cultural differences (e.g., gender, age, race, ethnic, and other cultural differences), the democratization of existing power structures, and the prevention of mass violence, which has erupted and is being fueled by religious and cultural differences. This chapter focuses upon the group practices of several gifted creative arts therapists and well-known artists whose group artwork possesses the potential to heal members of the cultural groups with whom they work.

The appeal of the basic encounter groups of the 1960s described in the previous chapter can be attributed to several factors: (a) these groups offered people a place to retreat to from the pressures and loneliness they experienced in their daily lives, (b) they provided participants with an opportunity to reflect upon the quality of their lives, and (c) they offered participants a chance to relate to one another in more humane, more transparent, and less defensive ways. The groups formed by creative arts therapists and artists described in this book also provide an opportunity for the development of *communitas*, in much the same way that encounter groups did for participants during the 1960s. However, one major differ-

ence that exists among art-making groups that share a healing intention
is that participants spend less time in providing each other verbal feedback about their interpersonal behavior and, instead, spend more time
interacting with one another through various modes of creative expression. Although art-making groups conducted by artists are formed with
the intention of creating collaboratively produced art objects or performance pieces that are meant to be shared publicly with outsiders, the
artworks generated within a group art-making process conducted by creative arts therapists are not meant for public display or to be judged for
their artistic merit, but rather serve a primarily mediative function within
the process of self- and communal healing.

Some of the healing functions that a group art-making process serves
for members who are undergoing difficult developmental or external
transitions are (a) the lowering of social barriers that exist among group
members, such as language differences and social role differences, (b) the
creation of group rituals that help group members negotiate societally
stigmatized life cycle transitions, (c) the creation of artistic symbols that
valorize and make explicit the cultural identities and histories of cultural
groups that have been marginalized by dominant cultural groups, (d) the
restoration of faith in the goodness of others and hope for a future tomorrow by victims who have been exposed to violent catastrophic events,
(e) the creation of public artworks that encourage peaceful dialogue and
conflict resolution among groups that possess different cultural identities
and worldviews, and (f) the creation of public artworks that enable a
nation to mourn and remember its collective physical and symbolic losses.

THE LOWERING OF LANGUAGE AND ROLE
SOCIAL BARRIERS

During the summer of 1990, I conducted a week-long psychodynamic
intensive dance/movement therapy workshop in Paris with a group of
about 14 French, Swiss German, and Italian mental health professionals.
This group taught me a great deal about overcoming some of the social
barriers that are imposed by language and by professional role affiliations
that a group of strangers born in different countries bring with them to
any social situation. Because all of the participants in the workshop spoke
fluent French and a little English, the French dance therapist who organized the workshop and I decided to use French as the language through
which the workshop would be conducted. However, because I do not
speak French fluently, she had to serve as my interpreter throughout the
workshop.

The workshop began with everyone present introducing themselves to one another. Then, when I was introduced by the interpreter, she mentioned that I pos-

sessed "a psychodynamic orientation to dance/movement therapy." After her introduction, some group members wanted to know more about my theoretical orientation. (In advance of the workshop, participants had been mailed a packet of readings that were intended to give them some sense of how I work as a dance/ movement therapist). Soon thereafter, a verbal argument broke out between some of the French participants with respect to the merit of the different theoretical positions with which each was affiliated as a mental health practitioner. Thus, the workshop began with group participants being polarized into competing professional role factions. When my French colleague whispered to me "that the French can argue endlessly about their theoretical positions," her comment provided me with a clue as to how I could proceed with this particular workshop. I decided to shift the participants' focus entirely upon their own somatic and movement experience of the moment to bypass their intellectual defenses over the anxiety they were experiencing in this novel and strange situation. I also made a mental note to myself that in this workshop I would limit all future theoretical discussions to one hour following the completion of the experiential component of the workshop.

Because of the time-limited nature of an intensive workshop's structure (daily sessions, each lasting for seven hours with a one-hour break for lunch, for a total of seven days), these events tend to be highly structured, and the major challenge for the practitioner becomes how to help participants find their own unique spontaneous gesture within the open-ended group structure that is provided by the therapist. Following is the outline of the open-ended movement structure that I provided during the first session of this workshop to acquaint participants' with their unique movement patterns, boundaries, and personal spaces and to encourage their relational openness toward others who shared certain similarities as well as certain differences with them. This outline is intended to give the reader some sense of how the language and role barriers that were encountered at the outset of the workshop were addressed through a creative movement process that focused on the subjective experience of each mover.

Attending to One's Bodily-Felt Experiencing

The workshop began with participants being encouraged to shift their attention to their own bodily-felt experiencing. They were encouraged to attend to whatever tensions, feelings, images, and thoughts came up for them and to find their own way of releasing whatever tension they discovered in various parts of their bodies by stretching, breathing, massaging, or moving in any way they chose that allowed them to release the tension they found in their bodies.

Exploring One's External Environment

Participants were then asked to explore the empty large studio space that they occupied as a group. Once standing, they were encouraged to follow their own impulse to move at their own pace and in whatever way they wished. As participants began to move in the large studio space, their attention was focused upon their surroundings. They were asked to attend to the size, textures, colors, and objects they found during their exploration of the studio space.

Discovering One's Own Immediate Movement Pattern

After participants became acquainted with their environment, their attention was returned to how they moved through the space they had just explored—they were encouraged to notice how much space they covered, how fast or slow they moved, the rhythms they created, the changes in direction they initiated, and the shapes their movements assumed as they moved through space. Next, they were encouraged to notice the kinds of movement patterns they created and to find "the one pattern that best reflects how you feel in the moment." Once participants found their own movement pattern, they were encouraged to make changes to their movement pattern at will as they continued moving through space. They were free to change their movement pattern in any way they felt like, but they were always "to return to the first pattern that they discovered to be their own."

Relating to Others While Not Losing One's Sense of Self

Once participants discovered their own unique way of moving in the moment and felt free to change this pattern while moving within the large studio space, they began to encounter other group participants who shared the same studio space with them. They were encouraged to notice others' movement patterns and "to sense some similarities and differences that they found from their own pattern." If they felt like it, they could acknowledge the presence of another through a movement gesture directed toward the other, but they were always to return to their own movement pattern. As participants began to interact with one another through movement, they became increasingly playful and began to risk engaging others through spontaneous movement improvisations and nonverbal pretend social playing.

Exploring One's Preconscious Subjective Experience

Once participants had an opportunity to move spontaneously with other participants, they were asked to search their environment for a specific place in the studio where they might be comfortable moving alone. Once there, they were asked to trace the size and shape of a space that they could regard as their own personal space, a space that belonged only to them, which no one could enter without their permission. They were encouraged to gradually close their eyes and begin to explore the interior of their personal space through movement—sensing its size, various textures, colors, and objects that they discovered while exploring the inside of their personal space. After some time elapsed, participants were given the option to linger inside their own personal space for as long as they wished, or, if they felt like, to leave their personal space altogether and allow themselves to explore the space that was outside of their personal space.

At some point, I observed that all of the participants had elected to venture out of their own personal space. From this point forward, I abstained from providing any further movement structure or suggestions, as I felt that whatever happened next needed to be entirely self-directed and to be created entirely by the participants themselves much in the way that illusory transitional objects are constructed by toddlers when they feel safe to play alone (see chapter 3 for a detailed discussion about the significance of transitional objects to human creativity).

I observed that all participants lay on the ground and that their movements seemed to be guided from within. Initially, their movements appeared to be triggered by their own bodily sensations and impulses and then to be guided by emergent mental images. As an outside observer, I could observe a high level of involvement with their internal sensations and images. Soon it appeared as though many of the participants assumed a movement identification with some type of animal drawn from their own imagination. The animals assumed the form of some type of sea animal that swims in the ocean. Some of the sea creatures began to swim toward other sea creatures that happened to be near them and to make contact with one another through movement. A few elected to simply move closer to other sea creatures without making any touch contact with them. Gradually, one by one, they all began to return to the space from which they had begun their ocean journey. When they returned to their own turf, they spontaneously began to make wailing sounds of all kinds. To me, the sounds they made were reminiscent of the sounds that whales make when they call out to one another under water. The harmonic and rhythmic patterns that they spontaneously created with one another through sound were quite extraordinary and otherworldly.

Returning to Ordinary Reality

When they ceased making sounds, they became perfectly still. After some time elapsed, I helped them to make the transition back from the deep receptive state that they had inhabited while on their ocean voyage back to the active, awake state from which they had begun their receptive movement journey. Their focus was returned once more to their own bodily-felt experience and to the connection that their bodies made with the ground beneath them that supported them. They were given some time "to reflect upon the journey (they) had just taken." As their awareness returned to the here and now of their experience, their eyes began to open. As they did so, they began to notice where they were in the studio and where other group members also were in the space. As their awareness returned to the present moment, they spontaneously began to gather themselves into a circle.

After some time elapsed, group members broke their silence and spoke. They began to comment spontaneously about the journey they had taken. A common thread that ran through all of the participants' comments was that they "had enjoyed getting to know each other without words." When they proceeded to describe the kinds of images that had emerged for them during the latter part of the session, many seemed surprised to discover that they had shared a particular image in common. Apparently, they all had allowed themselves to become temporarily transformed into "some kind of real or imaginary female sea mammal" (be it a siren, a dolphin, or another type of underwater female sea mammal). One group member described her experience in terms of "swimming in the midst of other females mammals from the same tribe." An impulse shared in common by all participants was their desire "to eventually return to my own island" while at the same time "wanting to stay connected with others from the same tribe who lived in other islands nearby."

By the end of the first session of this workshop, the interpersonal atmosphere that existed between the participants had shifted dramatically, from an initial defensive, verbal combative one, to a more receptive, nonverbal one, in which each participant felt free to be her own unique self without being threatened by the presence of others from the same tribe. To me, it seemed that the group was now ready to explore further their own subjective internal symbolic world and the intersubjective relational space they occupied with other group members through movement.

One explanation that can be offered for the shared archetypal image of a "female sea mammal from the same tribe" that emerged among workshop participants is that, at some point, all of the participants were able to become synchronous with each other's subjective experience. Redmond (1997) has noted that when people are in a receptive state of consciousness, they begin to share similar rhythmic sounds (I would add that they also begin to share similar movement patterns), and both hemispheres of their brains begin to operate at the same synchronized rhythm. She has also pointed out that pre-Christian religions intuitively made use of rhythmic chanting and dancing to induce the transcendent experience that seems to be associated with such hemispheric brain synchronization. In an empirical process study I conducted on the psychodynamic process of two long-term dance/movement therapy groups, I found that, over time, participants became increasingly better attuned to each other's nonverbal expressions, as indicated by their making direct eye contact, moving physically and emotionally closer to one another, and creating synchronous movement patterns with one another (Dosamantes, 1990, 1992).

In the Paris dance/movement therapy workshop that I conducted, once participants were able to get in touch with their own bodily-felt experience and to discover their own movement pattern of the moment, they were able to risk venturing out into the larger social environment inhabited by other group participants who exhibited different movement patterns. Finding the social environment to be nonthreatening made it possible for participants to risk entering the internal realm of their own imagination and to discover the boundaries and content of this personal space. Discovering what their internal world was like allowed participants to explore "the intersubjective world" occupied by others. As participants connected with one another while in a receptive, less conscious state, they were able to collaborate in the creation of symbols that reflected their shared collective feminine unconscious, which, in this instance, took on the archetypal form of a "female sea mammal." By the end of their movement journey, workshop participants appeared to be less fearful of losing themselves while interacting with others whom they originally viewed to be very different from themselves.

A receptive movement journey of the type I have described seems to offer participants a direct way of making contact with their own physical and emotional state of the moment. It appears to facilitate participants' open exploration of less conscious, unknown aspects of their subjective self-experience, which, in turn, allows them to risk reaching out to others who are different from themselves and to discover and touch their shared humanity. Such a journey allows group participants to transcend their tendency to view others as less human than themselves.

FORMS AND EXPRESSIONS OF POWER

Hillman (1995) has observed that our Western, contemporary understanding of power currently tends to be conceived in terms of two polarized kinds of power, expressed in absolute terms: as either a kind of absolute hierarchical power in which those who have the greatest access to available resources dominate and subordinate those who have less access to the same resources, or as an absolute populist kind of power that seeks to level all differences that exist among people by ruthlessly demanding conformity to sameness no matter what the circumstances might be. Neither of these kinds of power does justice to the broad, expressive range that humans are capable of engaging in when negotiating their various needs, from influential to coercive, from persuasive to violent, from legitimately acquired to usurped by manipulation or force, from mandated by symbol to enforced by weapons, from shared to absolute. Furthermore, power is located in persons, groups, and institutions. It can be used for constructive or destructive ends, depending upon the needs and motives of the persons and institutions who wield it.

As members of a capitalist, Western, modernist society that prizes democracy, we are often conflicted between our idealization of the democratic principles that underlie our elected form of government, and our adherence to a pragmatic, capitalist economic system. We enact these contradictory values in the public proclamations that we make in praise of populist and democratic values while simultaneously behaving in various areas of our lives in ways that profit us as individuals and ensure our dominance or superiority over other people. In the United States, groups that have the greatest access to available resources also wield the greatest power. Dominant groups get to set the rules, frame the social discourse, and label those who possess less power (Lott, 2002). In a hierarchical power structure, powerful groups stand to benefit from their ability to label those who possess less power than they do (Unger, 2000).

Some of the destructive consequences that can result when hierarchical power is applied in absolute terms are the exclusion, delegitimization, and marginalization of outside groups based on social status differentials ascribed to economic class, age, gender, race, ethnicity, sexual preference, religious, or other kinds of cultural differences. By first labeling members of less powerful groups as nonentities, expendable, and underserving, the label itself can subsequently be used by those who wield the greatest power to justify their discriminatory practices against others with less power.

RESPONDING TO CULTURAL DIFFERENCES: THE LIGHT AND THE DARK SIDE

The Art-Making Process to Heal and to Resist Ageism

One's identification with a marginalized cultural group can be a source of great personal pride. It can also fuel one's resistance against being arbitrarily stigmatized and oppressed by more dominant cultural groups. This section explores how artists and art therapists have made use of a group art-making process to valorize the cultural identities of groups that have been marginalized and rendered invisible by more dominant cultural groups.

One cultural group that is particularly stigmatized and oppressed in our society is the elderly. Butler (1987) defines ageism as a process of systematically stereotyping and discriminating against people on the basis of age. According to Schuster and Ashburn (1992), the elderly do not object to growing old, only to the discriminatory social practices that are leveled against them that result in their earning inadequate incomes, receiving mediocre health care, and obtaining substandard housing.

Aging is a difficult transition for both sexes to mediate, but it is a particularly difficult developmental transition to make by older women living in contemporary Western societies. In these societies, a woman's climacteric signals a serious life crisis for which there are no commonly accepted or shared rites of passage (Weigle, 1982). No longer able to fill the role of birthgiver, no longer viewed as an object of sexual desire, and deprived of the roles she once filled among pre-patriarchal tribal communities, that of wise woman and healer, the older Western American woman has been rendered invisible and useless by dominant cultural groups (Walker, 1985). Furthermore, because her presence is a reminder to others of their own mortality, she bears the additional burden of serving as a projection object for those who fear and are anxious about their own mortality and the prospect of dying.

These misogynist attitudes are a legacy left over by Christianity from the time of the Inquisition and from times when the witchcraft mania prevailed in the West (Dosamantes-Beaudry, 2001; Walker, 1985). These attitudes have not yet been totally eradicated and still persist in various veiled forms among contemporary Western societies. Today, however, an increasing number of older Western women are actively resisting being stigmatized and made invisible by virtue of their age. Many of them have turned to the archetype of the crone as a symbol of older woman's wisdom, willfulness, and strength (Le Guin, 1976).

Walker (1985) contends that the term "crone" is related to the word "crown." During pre-Christian times, the crone represented "the power of the ancient matriarch to make moral and legal decisions for her subjects and descendents" (p. 14). During contemporary times, the crone has become the archetypal symbol for the wise old woman who acknowledges and dares to assert her own authority and manages to transcend her detractors. What she has learned from life experience and how she carries herself through the world has been aptly described by Bly and Woodman (1998):

The crone knows the truth has set her free. . . . she is not willing to please for the sake of pleasing . . . nor is she looking for applause. . . . Always somewhere in the deepest hems of her skirts, she carries her Baba Yaga mortar and pestle. Everyday she will need them to process new energy. She knows that all the information in her head, all the rationalizations, all the polarities—all will have to be ground through her crucible, if they are to be embodied in her sacred body. Her big tears and her big Budha laugh make her a good companion in life (p. 206).

Today, many older women who lead Western, modernist lifestyles are succeeding in negotiating the difficult life cycle of senescence with confidence, dignity, and self-respect. One woman who is currently involved in the negotiation of this developmental transition is renowned modern dancer, choreographer, and UCLA professor emerita Marion Scott. In her seventies, she began to conceive a series of dances that she called *Spirit Dances*.

According to Marion, spirit dancing is a way of moving that invites each dancer to "let spirit in, in his or her own way" (Scott, 2002). The mover is guided by spirit rather than by any type of technique. In an interview I conducted with her about her current work, and about a piece she created in particular, *Spirit Dances 2—The Crones: A Celebration of Life*, she described her role as a choreographer not as someone who creates a preset series of movement patterns for her dancers to execute, but, rather, as someone who provides an open structure within which an event can occur. Within such an open structure, dancers are free to allow spirit to enter or not. The challenge for dancers lies in the fact that "one cannot control spirit." Spirit dancing is challenging because it is preconscious and unpredictable. "There is an edge to it that is frightening because you don't know in advance how it is going to go. It lives in the moment."

When she conceived *Spirit Dances 2—The Crones: A Celebration of Life*, all of the dancers whom she invited to participate were experienced performers, and ranged in age from 50 to 82 years, with the exception of the young male drummer who participated in the dance performance. The dance that these performers created collaboratively was scheduled to be performed three times publicly at Highways, an intimate performance venue, located in Santa Monica, California.

The performers selected included four dancers who were familiar with a particular dance form (e.g., modern dance, Indian, Javanese, and African dance), two professional actresses, and two musicians: a sound healer and a drummer. Commenting on the fact that the performers also differed with respect to body size and shape, Marion stated that "there was a time in this country, when older dancers and dancers of a certain size and shape would never have been allowed to perform publicly. Now it is possible" (Scott, 2002). The dancers met initially to get to know each other and to become comfortable performing for one another as well as to become familiar with "calling spirit" (Scott, 2002).

When I asked Marion what inspired her dance, she responded:

We are all actively involved in aging and dying. We are readying for whatever lies beyond life. Handicaps were also an important part of this piece. While facing our own mortality, it is important to go on despite our handicaps. In a culture that emphasizes youth, beauty and material things, the spiritual is not considered until you get older. Many people move towards spirituality only during the second half of their lives. Then, spirituality comes to the forefront (Scott, 2002).

The following is a brief description of the first performance of *Spirit Dances 2—The Crones: A Celebration of Life*, which I had an opportunity to attend.

The dance takes place within a garden setting during daylight. The musicians enter the stage and their music sets a spiritual tone for the performances to follow. Marion enters the stage first and invites the other performers to join her. A gossiping circle is formed while the performers wait for the last guest to arrive. When Nzingha arrives, the group is complete and the performance can begin. A series of solo performances follow.

Allegra begins the performance by acknowledging the musicians. She seems to use the music played by them as source of inspiration. She picks up a rain stick, an instrument that makes cascading sounds, and sways with it from side to side. As she continues swaying, she lifts her arms above her head and shakes them while appearing to be concentrating on conjuring spirit. As she moves, she seems to be comfortable in asserting her strength and authority.

She is followed by Leonora, who begins to make short, staccato sounds as she moves. At first, the squeaky sounds she makes sound like those that one might associate with small animals. Then the sounds she continues to make become transformed into sounds that a small child might make. Finally, she converts the sounds she is making into the words, "I was a little girl and now I am getting bigger . . . I am as old as I want to be." The audience roars with laughter. She begins to play off the energy that she receives from the audience. As she continues her monologue, she says, "I'll never leave, you'll have to push me off the stage."

Herta, the oldest performer of the group, moves next to the center of the stage. She appears to be a bit disoriented and looks toward Marion for direction. She moves, taking small tentative steps, and looks toward the audience for approval. She doesn't seem to know when to stop moving or when to get off center stage until Medha prompts her to do so.

She is followed by Kabbalah, the sound healer, who lifts a small bowl above her head. As Kabbalah begins to move through space, she uses the bowl to make wide circular movements in space. As she does so, she begins to make deep and low guttural sounds that help to generate a spiritual and mournful atmosphere. She seems to be using the bowl as a symbol of her own feminine spirit.

Medha follows her. She takes the bowl from Kabbalah and places it on the ground. Barefooted, she begins to stomp on the ground and quickly proceeds to move through the Indian dance forms that she has mastered so well, until suddenly her movement seems to come to an abrupt halt. It seems that, suddenly, "spirit" has left her, and, saddened by the break in her concentration, she becomes detached.

Nanik, a Javanese dancer, begins to slither like a snake on her belly onto the ground. She very quickly enters into a trance state, in which she seems to connect with some dark spirit that does not appear to frighten her. As she moves, she reaches toward other members of the group, making contact with them only through touch.

When she stops moving, Marion leaves the chair upon which she has been sitting and very tentatively moves onto the floor and begins to get in touch with "spirit." As she continues to maintain her focus on "spirit," she starts to create a variety of undulating hip and arm movements that appear to put her in touch with a sensual, feminine aspect of herself. Before returning to her chair, her whole body shudders.

She is followed by Jamaiel, the drummer, who addresses each of the participants through his drumming rhythms. (This experience is unusual for him. Ordinarily, as the drummer for the African dance classes that he accompanies, he sets the rhythm that the dancers will follow. In this context, he has to follow the rhythm that is set by each of the crone performers.)

Nzingha is the last performer. She places a long scarf on the ground and then raises it to the sky. She then connects with each performer through the scarf. She uses her scarf as an intermediary symbolic object between herself and each of the performers. After she dances with each member of the group, she creates her own solo dance with the scarf. The dance she creates takes her into an altered state that is charged with a great deal of energy. Soon, she begins to jump and leap up into the air. The performers as well as the entire audience become captivated and get swept away by her explosive energy. All present, including the audience, join her

Photo 6.1   *Spirit Dances 2—The Crones: A Celebration of Life,* conceived and directed by Marion Scott, Highways Performance Space, Los Angeles, May 5–7, 2000. Photograph from video by Adrian Ravarour.

in the celebratory atmosphere that she has helped to generate (see Photo 6.1). The dance concludes as the other performers encircle Nzingha and acknowledge her as being the heart of their circle. As the dance ends, the dancers raise their arms to the sky in triumphant celebration. The audience breaks out into loud spontaneous applause that continues for a long time.

As a member of the audience, I was particularly moved by the courage shown by each of the performers in risking finding or not finding spirit, and in exposing her physical and mental frailties so directly before an audience. After I left the theater, what remained with me was the conviction and hope that as I enter senescence, I will have the courage to confront my own mortality with the same dignity, humor, and compassion that each performer showed that evening in *Spirit Dances 2—The Crones: A Celebration of Life.*

CELEBRATING CULTURAL DIVERSITY AND PROMOTING INTERCULTURAL CONFLICT RESOLUTION

A major psychological problem confronting the world today is how can we acknowledge each other's cultural differences while simultaneously maintaining peaceful relationships with members of cultural groups who possess different cultural identities from our own, or how we can achieve "a world in balance" (Roth, 1991, p. 10). Judith Francisca Baca is an internationally acclaimed artist whose Chicana cultural heritage and political activist perspective have led her to seriously address both of these large social concerns through the contemporary murals and other public artworks that she creates. Baca is a cofounder and artistic director of SPARC (Social and Public Art Resource Center), a nonprofit organization dedicated to the production of public artworks. Debra J.T. Padilla, executive director of SPARC, describes this organization as

a politically spirited, socially relevant and diversity driven community based arts' organization.... At the heart of what we believe is that art is a tool for social change and self transformation. SPARC works are never simply individually authored endeavors, but rather a collaboration between artists and local residents, resulting in art which rises from within the community rather than being imposed upon it (Padilla, 2002).

Baca is also a professor with the UCLA Cesar Chavez Center and World Arts and Cultures Department. The murals that she creates follow in the tradition established by such renowned Mexican artists as Diego Rivera, David Alfaro Siqueiros, and Jose Clemente Orozco during Mexico's post-revolutionary era. She creates monumental public works of art whose construction involves a collective of people drawn from the ethnic communities to be depicted: other artists, local residents and students, experts in ethnic history, and technical staff drawn from these communities and from SPARC.

Baca views the mission of public art within contemporary society to be that of educating its members about what it means to live in a democracy. Her artwork always explores the relationship that exists between the site where the artwork is to be constructed and the history of the people about whom the artwork is to be created. Through the murals that she creates collaboratively with various constituencies, Baca validates the cultural identity as well as cultural history of members of ethnic groups who have been marginalized and oppressed by the dominant cultural groups.

In 1974, she was contacted by the Army Corps of Engineers in Los Angeles and commissioned to design a mural for a segment of the Tujunga Wash, a concrete river drainage channel that stretches for over a half a mile along the San Fernando Valley. When she stood at the site of the concrete wall that was to be painted and contemplated what it might become, she initially saw the concrete channel in terms of a metaphor as "a scar where the river once ran" (Baca, 2002, p. 15). This initial metaphor, in turn, gave rise to a second metaphor, "a tattoo on the scar where the river once ran," which came to guide her conception for *The Great Wall of*

Los Angeles (Baca, p. 15). The magnitude of the project she conceived required the efforts of many people possessing different kinds of skills and knowledge:

The Great Wall of Los Angeles production began with 80 youth recruited though the juvenile justice system and paid by a program to employ economically disadvantaged young people. When completed this project employed over 400 youth along with 40 historians, 40 artists, hundreds of historical witnesses and thousands of residents involved in the production of a half-mile narrative mural. The work became a monument to interracial harmony as methods were developed to work across the differences of race and class. As a result, relationships were formed that are now 25 years long (Baca, p. 15).

The site where *The Great Wall of Los Angeles* came to be built became a safe heaven for youth who came from different Los Angeles' neighborhoods. Youth assembled at the site without fear of reprisals from rival gangs. Because of its location and its length, the wall itself provided a natural site where a historical narrative of epic proportions could be constructed. What was unique about this public artwork was that it presented an alternative view of the ethnic history of Los Angeles. Depicted on the wall was the local history of people of color whose history has been distorted or omitted in the public school history books (see Photo 6.2).

Photo 6.2   Long-shot black and white photograph of *The Great Wall of Los Angeles*, mural conceived and produced by Judith F. Baca, Los Angeles, 1975.

The youth employed to work on *The Great Wall of Los Angeles* were supervised by professional artists who worked closely with them from four to eight hours per day. The youth also received instruction in art and in the ethnic history of Los Angeles. They also engaged in improvisational theater workshops aimed at teaching them to work collaboratively with other people from different cultural groups (Olympic Arts Festival in Los Angeles, 1984).

As the director for the project, Baca overcame the youth's tendency to behave in ethnocentric ways by encouraging them to work closely inter-culturally with members from different ethnic groups. She states:

It was important for me when I got the group together to represent each of the ethnic groups and then put them into a whole, and to move them between learning about each others' cultures so that Chicano kids were not encouraged to work only on Chicano history (Pohl, 1996, p. 230).

The following comment describes some of the intercultural problems that she encountered as a result of the great diversity that the youth brought to the project:

The problem with the group as we came together had to do with communication, cultural misunderstandings that came from long histories of not having lived and worked together with each other. For example, there were different ways that people spoke to each other. There were also differences in body language. One group included gang-identified kids, kids who had recently fled Cambodia, and fourteen-year old expecting mothers, just to give an idea of the range (Galindo, 2001, p. 2).

In addressing the significance that *The Great Wall of Los Angeles* holds for Southern California, Rickey (1981) maintains that its most significant contribution lies in its telescoping of the history of Southern California by showing the experience and contributions made by various indigenous and immigrant ethnic groups: "It is a monumentally scaled history de-picting the panorama of events that contributed to Los Angeles' distinc-tive profile" (p. 87). In the future, Baca plans to repair damaged parts of the wall, to include missing decades, and to add new images drawn from the new millennium.

Another public artwork conceived by Baca in the late 1980s was in-spired by a group of peace activists based in Los Angeles. She envisioned a traveling mural installation that would inspire debates about issues that might contribute to world peace. Based on meetings with a cross-section of scholars, visionaries, artists, and students, complex images and narra-tives began to emerge in her mind that became focused on the thematic metaphor of "a vision of the future without fear." The completed instal-

Photo 6.3   Black and white photograph of *The World Wall*, traveling mural, Finland Installation, conceived and produced by Judith F. Baca, Joensuu, Finland, 1996.

lation consists of eight murals, each 10 feet by 30 feet, to be known as *The World Wall* (Roth, 1991). *The World Wall* premiered in Joensuu, Finland, and then traveled to Gorky Park, in Moscow. The mural installation is semicircular in shape. It gives the impression of a set of extended arms extended to welcome those who would gather to dialogue and deliberate about world peace within its circumscribed space. The panels placed on the inside of the installation were conceived by Judith herself, and those that appear on the outside of the installation were meant to be created by international artists from other countries (see Photo 6.3).

Recently, Baca was invited by the Durango Latino Education Coalition in Colorado to create a mural that would help to reduce the intense conflict that had been generated in recent years between youth factions that came from three diverse cultural groups (Ute, Latino, and Anglo). This coalition was interested in bringing students from these three cultures together "to create something bigger than themselves" and "to deal with the issue of conflict straight on" (Reed, 2002).

Baca asked students from each of these groups to select geographical landmarks that held special significance for them and their communities, to draw images about their cultural histories, and to contribute photographs that reflected their own personal histories with their families. The

Photo 6.4   Black and white photograph of unfinished *La Memoria de Nuestra Tierra Durango,* mural conceived and produced by Judith F. Baca, Durango and Los Angeles, 2002.

mural, *La Memoria de Nuestra Tierra Durango* (the memory of our land Durango), is a collage of the diverse personal and cultural histories that were submitted by the students superimposed upon the various Durango landmarks that hold special significance for each cultural group (see Photo 6.4).

Baca was able to combine the multiple images that she received from the students through the use of new computer technology. The students themselves took the conceptual plan to the city's project planning commission and council. During a three-year-long process, Baca met several times in person with each of the student groups. The ideas, drawings, and photographs contributed by each student group were then sent to her in Los Angeles. In her computer lab in Los Angeles, she blended these multiple images to create the larger vision that she had for the project. She wanted to inscribe the personal images submitted by the students into the various Durango landmarks that held special meaning for each cultural group (e.g., the depiction of a Ute mother and child was superimposed upon the image of Silver Peak, a mountain that holds special sacred meaning for the entire Ute tribe).

The completed mural is a 20 foot by 35 foot mural that hangs on the exterior of the city's art center. *La Memoria de Nuestra Tierra Durango* depicts the diverse personal and cultural histories of each cultural group that has made Durango what it has become. The mural offers material evidence of each ethnic group's contribution to the city's cultural history and creates a new, more comprehensive and positive narrative of the personal and cultural history of all of Durango's inhabitants (Reed, 2002).

THE DARK SIDE OF CULTURAL IDENTITY

Although the arts can serve to highlight the best that diverse cultural groups have to contribute to our multicultural society, power differences associated with cultural differences can often serve as a catalyst for social divisiveness. Whenever people feel that they do not belong and that their religion, nationality, race, or ethnicity are under attack, even mass murder can be rationalized and legitimized (Maalouf, 2002). Although the root causes of war and mass murder are more likely to lie with tyranny, greed for territory, wealth, and absolute power, "identity" is "what gets peoples' blood boiling" (Buruma, 2002, p. 12). It is what makes one cultural group do unspeakable things to another cultural group. When the world is reduced to us versus them (e.g., Germans vs. Jews, Hindus vs. Muslims, Hutus vs. Tutsies), only mass murder will do. It becomes easy to rationalize that "we can only survive, if they are slaughtered" (Buruma, p. 12).

PERSUADING NORMAL PEOPLE TO COMMIT EVIL DEEDS

In the aftermath of the violence that took place on September 11, 2001, Phillip Zimbardo (2001), president of the American Psychological Association, warned against our tendency to demonize terrorists as an "alien breed" in light of the findings from past social psychological research that demonstrates the ease and rapidity with which normal people can be induced to engage in harmful behavior against others, when urged to do so by an authority figure whom they respect.

The first of these social psychological experiments was conducted by Milgram (1974) at Yale University in 1963. This researcher (a respected authority figure) was able to induce a group of volunteer male undergraduates, ostensibly recruited to participate in a memory experiment and assigned to the role of teacher, to administer life-threatening levels of shock to a male undergraduate who had been assigned to the role of student (who enacted being shocked). The second social psychology experiment essentially replicated Milgram's findings within a different context. In 1971 at Stanford University, Zimbardo and Harvey (1974) were able to induce normal male undergraduate volunteers, recruited to participate in a mock prison ward experiment and randomly assigned to the role of guard, to behave in bullying, sadistic ways toward other normal male undergraduate volunteers, randomly assigned to the role of prisoner, at the urging of the prison warden (the experimenter). On the sixth day of running the experiment, the researchers involved with this research project felt compelled to abruptly terminate the experiment for the good of all concerned.

These two social psychology experiments demonstrate the ease with which ordinary, normal men can be persuaded to commit harmful acts of violence toward those who are cast in less powerful roles than themselves, at the urging of a respected male authority figure. It shows the ease with which someone characterized as "the other" can be transformed into a nonentity, dehumanized, and tortured under the direction of an admired authority figure. To avert the escalation of violence between groups, it seems imperative that we find ways to assume responsibility for our own individual behavior and reclaim our own fears and prejudices toward persons who are different from ourselves.

After the events of September 11, 2001, Zimbardo (2001) suggested several strategies that might help nurture our tolerance toward outside groups: (a) identifying those situational elements that can lead even good people to engage in evil deeds, (b) acknowledging the dark side of religion and how religiously based value systems can be perverted to justify and reward the most heinous of human deeds, (c) individually and collectively refusing to adopt the terrorists' devaluing of human life, and (d) nurturing tolerance, compassion, and justice toward all people.

HEALING LIVES FRACTURED BY WAR AND RESTORING A SENSE OF HOPE IN THE FUTURE

Under the sponsorship of a British charity, War Child, two art therapists, Debra Kalmanowitz and Bobby Lloyd, traveled to the former Yugoslavia in 1994 to conduct art therapy pilot programs at two refugee war camps in Croatia and Slovania. These art therapists referred to their work as a "portable studio," based on their belief that artwork can take place anywhere, inside or outside of buildings, and even in a town dump.

Kalmanowitz and Lloyd (1999) believe that exposure to the ravages of war can make people feel less than human and that a healing art-making process can help war refugees restore their humanity and sense of hope. The therapeutic art-making process followed by these art therapists proceeded from the war refugees' becoming familiar with the art materials that were offered within the context of a nonjudgmental environment, to learning to portray their unspeakable emotions and thoughts through visual means, to gaining access to memories and experiences represented in the images that they created, to working through and labeling their experiences, and to finally rejoining the world. The art therapists felt that the art therapy sessions they brought to the refugee war camps "needed to serve as a vessel strong enough to hold whatever arose" (Kalmanowitz & Lloyd, p. 23).

The first war refugee camp they worked at was located in Slovania. The refugees at this camp were primarily women and children. Art-making at this refugee war camp took on many forms for the various generations present. Although the mothers would not attend art sessions, they were willing to attend embroidery sessions, the grandparents who attended sessions showed a keen interest in making portrait paintings of their partners, and children, who constituted the largest group at the camp, became very invested in building, tearing down, and rebuilding a semblance of "home." Commenting on the meaning that the creation of home held for these children, Kalmanowitz and Lloyd (1999) state:

The building of the houses created a structure in which the children could play, create and imagine. Issues such as ownership and authorship, finding one's place placing oneself inside it, became crucial and were usually resolved through the activity (p. 19).

The second war refugee camp was in Croatia. This refugee camp housed primarily traumatized children and single mothers. The experience of the art therapists at this site proved to be far more difficult for the art therapists because the level of trauma experienced by the refugees at this camp left them devastated, empty, and extremely needy. The refugees expressed this need by demanding more of everything material from the art therapists: art materials, coffee, cigarettes, and even the therapists' personal possessions.

In another part of the world, under the auspices of the Israeli Community Stress Prevention Centre, drama therapist Mooli Lahad and his colleagues became involved in organizing a number of crisis intervention drama therapy groups for the temporary evacuees of the town of Kiryat Shmona, a town that had been exposed to continuous rocket shelling by a Lebanese group that lasted 16 days.

According to Lahad (1999), the majority of the members of these groups were normal people having normal reactions to abnormal situations. Consequently, the primary objectives of the groups that he formed included the restoration of the residents' self-confidence and trust in their ability to cope with the circumstances that they faced, and the development of a sense of community or belonging by cultivating the knowledge that others cared and were there to offer support.

An attempt was made to form time-limited groups on the basis of culturally homogeneous groups: four shelter groups, one group of blind people, two groups of single parents, one group of Russian immigrants, one group of community workers, one group of the staff of a hostel for mentally disabled, and one group of volunteers who supported the community workers during times of disaster.

The structure followed by each of these groups incorporated a blending of some of the methods borrowed from various creative arts therapies modalities. For instance, each meeting began with a series of warm-up physical exercises, followed by some creative activity such as drawing, writing, sculpting, story making, dramatic improvisations, and role play-ing. Through these activities, a theme or issue would emerge that could be further explored and processed. This was followed by a closure ritual.

According to Lahad (1999), a significant component of the process that unfolded in all groups involved the creation of ceremonies and rituals. Certain visual symbols proved to be particularly useful in the creation of healing metaphors. For example, the image of "a rope" conjured up the metaphors of "returning," "uniting," "untying knots," and "connecting loose ends." The image of "a stick" proved to be useful with blind people who used the visual symbol to create the metaphor of "path finding." The visual images of "baskets" and "boxes" served as useful metaphors for "containers of the group members' worries," for "things to pack for an evacuation," for "putting things in" or for "getting stuff out." Among the neighborhood shelter groups, "the forest" proved to be a useful symbol with which to describe "a place where the unknown prevails but at the same time one can meet challenges," "encounter fears," "learn to survive," and "make new friends."

Feedback obtained from group participants indicated that many wel-comed the intimacy that was generated within these groups and were grateful for the support that they received from other group members. Participants also found these groups to be helpful in relieving tension and in learning from others about how to cope with difficult circumstances. They were able to experience firsthand the resourcefulness and the poten-tial for resilience that everyone possesses.

GRIEVING AND MOURNING GROUP LOSSES

Loss and grief are universal and inevitable experiences of our human existence. Both of these processes begin at birth and continue throughout the human life cycle. They are complex experiences that reach to the heart of what it means to be a human being—to experience, to reflect upon one's vulnerability, and to care about others (Schuster & Ashburn 1992). Loss and grief serve as powerful agents for change because they force us to reexamine the ways in which we conduct our lives and they challenge us to consider anew the meaning and purpose of life itself.

Loss can be defined as the subjective experience of being without some-thing one has had (Peretz, 1970). Deprivation always results from a sense of loss. Whether consciously acknowledged or not, loss has a powerful emotional impact upon our sense of self and sense of security in the world. It therefore requires some type of adaptation. This adaptation takes the form of a grieving process that either proceeds to a successful resolution or becomes blocked in some major way that winds up diminishing the quality of one's life.

Losses have been described by developmental psychologists in terms of various dichotomous categories (e.g., physical vs. symbolic and maturational vs. situational). Physical losses involve tangible deprivation (e.g., the actual loss of a loved one); symbolic losses refer to abstract kinds of deprivation (e.g., the loss of social status). Maturational losses are associated with the process of growth and development. They are generally anticipated and predictable and are associated with developmental transitions. Situational losses are unpredictable and unanticipated and generally accompany external transitions.

Grief is a response to any type of experienced loss. Its duration and intensity depends upon the value of the lost object. Although grief is the internal reaction to loss, mourning is the external or public expression of loss (Schuster & Ashburn, 1992). A comparison of mourning rituals manifested across 80 different cultures performed by Rosenblatt, Walsh, and Jackson (1976) showed that, although crying seemed to be a critical component of all mourning practices in these cultures, how grief was permitted outward expression also varied depending upon a culture's worldview, values, attitudes, expectations, rituals, and the customs it practiced.

Critical to the success of "grief work" is the availability of support systems one has during the length of the grieving process. Although grief does not follow a predictable pattern, the prevailing attitude of a society toward death, loss, and mourning can dramatically influence a person's ability or inability to achieve partial or complete resolution or to experience a prolonged grieving process (Joyce, 1984).

One way that societies have to memorialize national losses is through the creation of illusory, public symbols that hold multiple layers of meaning for the members of a given society. For example, when Yitzhak Rabin, the prime minister of Israel, was assassinated, not only was the sense of political stability of this nation shattered, but also the hopes of all who had hoped for a peaceful resolution to the Middle East crisis.

In the midst of these bleak events, many young people who otherwise were not connected as a group spontaneously began to gather together to create a temporary mourning community within which to cope with the physical loss of their leader as well as the symbolic loss of their hopes for peace that he had come to represent for them. Klingman, Shalev, and Pearlman (2000) report that immediately following Rabin's death in 1995, many Israeli youth gathered together in Tel Aviv's city square to transform this public meeting space into a site for mourning and remembrance. They did so by resorting to drawing graffiti upon the city's walls:

The graffiti produced immediately after Rabin's assassination created a kind of collectivism that may have allowed individuals to cope in the face of a bleak situation by actively developing an expressive ritual of fellowship, which affirmed that one was not alone in grief, anger, shame or in feeling helplessness (Klingman et al., 2000, p. 300).

The most frequent symbols that appeared in the graffiti that was spontaneously produced by these youth were two international symbols—the peace sign and the peace dove—and two national symbols—the Star of David and the Israeli flag. The peace sign significantly outweighed all other symbols (Klingman et al., 2000). In this context, the public sharing of graffiti symbols with other youth of their generation became a vehicle that allowed these Israeli youth to express their deepest aspirations and hopes for a peaceful future.

HEALING CULTURALLY STIGMATIZED LOSSES

All societies appear to need symbolic objects through which to represent, communicate, encode, and stimulate the recall of significant shared cultural events (Roberts & Roberts, 1996). In Western societies, members make use of both written texts as well as material objects to recall and revise their personal and collective histories and to mourn their collective losses (e.g., through historical documents, books, photographs, paintings, sculptures, monuments, poems, dances, and musical scores).

The creation of national symbols helps a nation mourn and remember its losses. This is a particularly critical psychological function served by national memorials, particularly when the losses that need to be mourned have been stigmatized or denied by dominant cultural groups. For example, because the Vietnam War conducted by the United States was not sanctioned by the nation as a whole, inadequate support was given to those who needed to grieve loved ones who died in that war. For many years following the Vietnam War, political and intellectual battles continued that significantly interfered with the survivors' need to complete their grieving process (Webb, 1985). Maya Lin's Vietnam Veterans' Memorial became a major instrument for facilitating the mourning process of an entire nation (Provost, 1989). Addressing the deeper, symbolic meaning that Lin's memorial held for Americans, art therapist Maxine Borowsky Junge (1999) commented:

The Wall is made of highly polished black granite which in effect, acts as a mirror. Here the living can see themselves superimposed upon the names of the dead. The names are represented chronologically instead of alphabetically, like a Greek epic representing the chronicle of war (p. 197).

The *AIDS Quilt* is another public artwork that became a symbol for stigmatized loss on a national scale. This quilt is made up of panels containing the names of those who have died of AIDS and was created by surviving loved ones as a means to grieve their losses and as an act of defiance against the victims being made invisible and forgotten. Junge (1999) offers an explanation about the significance that this material object of memorialization holds for our nation: "Naming provides relief through telling a history that has been taboo. It embodies the act of bearing witness" (p. 198).

SUMMARY OF GROUP VIGNETTES

The public sphere of psychosocial relationships is where we construct our cultural identities, and where members of various cultural groups contest and negotiate problematic group social concerns that matter to them. This sphere is where we come to terms with ways to restore our collective balance when natural and man-made catastrophes such as hurricanes, fire, earthquakes, terrorism, and war threaten to cause mass destruction and chaos in people's lives. The group vignettes cited in this chapter have illustrated some ways in which the healing potential of an art-making process has been used by some creative arts therapists and artists to reduce intracultural and intercultural conflict and to promote a sense of *communitas* among members of different cultural groups.

The intensive workshop I conducted in Paris with a group of mental health professionals showed how a nonverbal experiential movement-based process enabled group participants to become better acquainted with the contents of their internal symbolic life and to gain a deeper, bodily-felt understanding of their own personal movement patterns, spaces, and boundaries, which, in turn, led to their becoming more open and less defensive toward other group members who differed from them with respect to language spoken and professional role played in the outside world.

The collaborative production of *Spirit Dances 2—The Crones: A Celebration of Life,* based on Marion Scott's concept of spirit dancing performed by older women master performers celebrated the complexity of what it means to be an older woman negotiating the last cycle of life within a patriarchal society in which ageist and misogynist attitudes still prevail. The inspired dancing of these master performers affirmed the collective wisdom, dignity, and strength of the crone archetype.

Large public artworks such as *The Great Wall of Los Angeles, The World Wall,* and *La Memoria de Nuestra Tierra Durango,* created by master muralist Judith F. Baca and her collaborators at SPARC, were driven by the needs of the communities that this community-based arts organization serves. SPARC seeks to democratize our society by valorizing the ethnic identities and the cultural histories of groups that have been marginalized by dominant cultural groups in our society. SPARC also aims to reduce the intercultural conflict that exists between various ethnic cultural groups and to create public artworks that will inspire meaningful international dialogue on ways to achieve global peace and restore the world to a more balanced state.

Social psychologists have documented the ease with which normal people can be persuaded to commit evil deeds by charismatic leaders who label outside groups as different and inferior, and thereby encourage acts of brutality against them (Milgram, 1974; Zimbardo, 2001). When people can be persuaded that outside groups are to blame for their problems and when they are convinced that their grievances cannot be resolved through peaceful dialogue, our human propensity for enemy making rises, and the world becomes a more dangerous place to be.

Art therapists Debra Kalmanowitz and Bobby Lloyd (1999) brought their portable studio to the war refugee camps of Slovania and Croatia in the former Yugoslavia. These art therapists worked to create a strong vessel in which the difficult transitions facing the war refugees could be negotiated. They helped to rekindle the war refugees' sense of hope and faith in others. Working under the most dire of circumstances, these art therapists took into account the special needs of the various constituencies they found at each of the camps. Drama therapist Mooli Lahad (1999) also helped to create many crisis intervention groups for the temporary evacuees of Kiryat Shmona in Israel, a town besieged by intensive and continuous rocket shelling. Through an art-making group process that blended many of the methods developed by various creative arts therapies, Lahad and the other group leaders who worked with him helped to restore the evacuees' trust in others and their hope for a better future.

Being able to grieve and mourn the losses that one sustains when sudden and unexpected catastrophic events occur that cause great chaos and loss of life is critical to the recovery of one's sense of going on being and to the restoration of one's trust in others. When the losses suffered touch an entire nation, its citizens are often compelled to create memorials in public spaces to mourn and to memorialize their collective losses. This is particularly critical when the losses suffered are controversial and highly socially contested. Following the death of their leader, many youth in Tel Aviv expressed their refusal to give up on their dream for a peaceful future by painting graffiti peace symbols on the walls of their public buildings (Klingman et al., 2000). Immediately following the catastrophic events of September 11, 2001, many Americans, too, were moved to create impromptu memorials to mourn their losses. As a collective, we turned to the arts to help us regain our faith in others, to revive our hope for a better tomorrow, and to strengthen our resolve to work toward decreasing intercultural conflict to restore the world to a more sane and balanced state.

The final chapter, chapter 7, summarizes the basic tenets underlying the developmental-relational arts-based model of healing introduced in this book. Several recommendations that might help make the healing power of the arts become more accessible to a wider spectrum of people are also made.

REFERENCES

Baca, J. F. (2002, January 14). Birth of a movement #1, *Judith F. Baca Reader, JB Archive,* pp. 1–32.

Bly, R., & Woodman, M. (1998). *The maiden king: The reunion of masculine and feminine.* New York: Henry Holt.

Buruma, I. (2002, April 11). The bloodlust of identity. *The New York Review, XLIX* (6), 12–14.

Butler, R. N. (1987). Ageism. In G. L. Maddox (Ed.), *The encyclopedia of aging* (pp. 22–23). New York: Springer.

Dosamantes, E. (1990). Movement and psychodynamic pattern changes in long-term dance/movement therapy groups. *American Journal of Dance Therapy, 12* (1), 27–44.

Dosamantes, I. (1992). Spatial patterns associated with the separation-individuation process in adult long-term psychodynamic movement therapy groups. *Arts in Psychotherapy Journal, 19,* 3–11.

Dosamantes-Beaudry, I. (2001). The suppression and modern re-emergence of sacred feminine healing traditions. *Arts in Psychotherapy Journal, 28* (1), 31–37.

Galindo, P. (2001, December 27). Judith F. Baca: Public artist, activist, youth mentor. *Judith F. Baca Reader, JB Archive,* pp. 1–6.

Hillman, J. (1995). *Kinds of power.* New York: Banton Doubleday Dell Publishing Group.

Joyce, C. (1984). A time for grieving. *Psychology Today, 18* (11), 42–46.

Junge, M. B. (1999). Mourning, memory and life itself: The AIDS Quilt and the Vietnam Veterans' Memorial Wall. *Arts in Psychotherapy Journal, 26* (3), 195–203.

Kalmanowitz, D., & Lloyd, B. (1999). Fragments of art at work: Art therapy in the former Yugoslavia. *Arts in Psychotherapy Journal, 26* (1), 15–25.

Klingman, A., Shalev, R., & Pearlman, A. (2000). Graffiti: A creative means of youth coping with collective trauma. *Arts in Psychotherapy Journal, 27* (5), 299–307.

Lahad, M. (1999). The use of drama therapy with crisis intervention groups, following mass evacuation. *Arts in Psychotherapy Journal, 26* (1), 27–33.

Le Guin, U. (1976, Summer). The space crone. *CoEvolution Quarterly,* pp. 108–110.

Lott, B. (2002). Cognitive and behavioral distancing from the poor. *American Psychology, 59* (2), 100–110.

Maalouf, A. (2002). *In the name of identity: Violence and the need to belong.* New York: Arcade Publishing.

Milgram, S. (1974). *Obedience to authority.* New York: Harper & Row.

Olympic Arts Festival in Los Angeles. (1984). *Walking Tour and Guide to the Great Wall of Los Angeles* (pp. 1–19). Los Angeles: Author.

Padilla, D.J.T. (2002, June 14). Personal communication. Los Angeles, CA.

Peretz, D. (1970). Development, object-relationships and loss. In B. Schoenberg, A. C. Carr, D. Peretz, & A. H. Kutschen (Eds.), *Loss and grief: Psychological management in medical practice* (pp. 3–19). New York: Columbia University Press.

Pohl, F. (1996). Judy Baca: Community and culture in the United States. *Women's Studies, 25,* 215–217.

Provost, P. K. (1989). Vietnam: Resolving the death of a loved one. *Archives of Psychiatric Nursing, 3,* 29–33.

Redmond, L. (1997). *When the drummers were women.* New York: Three Rivers Press.

Reed, I. (2002, May 6). Heritage mural "reCollections" installed at Durango Arts Center. *Four Corners Business Journal,* pp. 1–3.

Rickey, C, (1981, May). The writing on the wall. *Los Angeles Today,* pp. 54–57.

Roberts, M. N., & Roberts, A. (1996). *Luba and the making of history.* New York: The Museum for African Art.

Rosenblatt, P. C., Walsh, R. P., & Jackson, D. A. (1976). *Grief and mourning in cross-cultural perspective.* New Haven, CT: H.R.A.F. Press.

Roth, M. (1991, November 14). Towards a world in balance. A conversation with Judy Baca: Part I. *Artweek,* pp. 10–11.

Scott, M. (2002, March 7). Personal communication. Los Angeles, CA.

Schuster, C., & Ashburn, S. (1992). *The process of human development.* Philadelphia: J. B. Lippincott.

Taylor, C. (1994). The politics of recognition. In D. T. Goldberg (Ed.), *Multiculturalism: A critical reader* (pp. 75–106). Malden, MA: Blackwell.

Unger, R. K. (2000). Outside inside: Positive marginality and social change. *Journal of Social Issues, 56,* 163–179.

Walker, B. G. (1985). *The Crone: Woman of age, wisdom and power.* San Francisco: Harper & Row.

Webb, J. (1985, April 6). Viet vets didn't kill babies and they aren't suicidal. *The Washington Post,* Section C, pp. 1, 2.

Weigle, M. (1982). *Spiders & spinsters: Women and mythology.* Albuquerque, NM: University of New Mexico Press.

Zimbardo, P. G. (November, 2001). Opposing terrorism by understanding the human capacity for evil. *Monitor on Psychology, 32* (10), 48–50.

Zimbardo, P. G., & Harvey, C., (1974). The psychology of imprisonment: Privation, power and pathology. In Z. Rubin (Ed.), *Doing unto others* (pp. 61–76). Englewood Cliffs, NJ: Prentice Hall.

CHAPTER 7

Recapitulation and Conclusions

A DEVELOPMENTAL-RELATIONAL ARTS-BASED MODEL OF HEALING

The arts have the potential to contribute significantly to the ways in which we respond to difficult developmental and external life transitions that demand major emotional and cognitive accommodations on our part. This is because when we have to cope with the depth and breadth of emotional disruption and chaos that such transitions wreak, our rational, pragmatic, material solutions simply are not sufficient or adequate to the task. During times of crisis, the arts possess the power to comfort us and to serve as a means of emotional release for us, but, most important, they possess the power to directly connect us to our inner symbolic life. This capacity enables us to perceive shadow aspects of our self-experience that we ordinarily find difficult to acknowledge and to claim as individuals or as members of a collective when functioning under the influence of our rational minds.

A therapeutic or healing art-making process makes possible a psychological journey into the mysteries of our internal symbolic world. As we start out on this journey, our awareness shifts from an active to a receptive state of consciousness. While in a receptive state, we are able to make direct contact with preconscious, sensory, and imaginal realms of experience and expression (Dosamantes-Alperson, 1979; Koestler, 1977). As the scope of our perceptual range is widened, our psychological defenses are temporarily deactivated. While in a receptive state, we are able to assume a relaxed, open, and playful attitude toward material objects that we encounter in the environment or symbolic objects that emerge from our imagination that hold emotional resonance for us. As we begin to identify and to interact with these objects through pretend play, we are able to unravel the special meaning they hold for us.

As human beings we inevitably encounter two kinds of psychosocial challenges during our lifetime: life cycle changes that are expected and generally occur gradually, and external, situational changes that occur suddenly and unexpectedly and often involve physical danger and violence. Our capacity to successfully negotiate developmental transitions makes it possible for us to comply with the demands of our society for age-appropriate comportment and behavior (Erikson, 1968). The more difficult the developmental transition to be negotiated is, the greater the likelihood that we will automatically undergo an involuntary or structural type of regression that phenomenologically returns us to the kinds of identifications and attachments styles we forged earlier during childhood with significant others. Consequently, the most difficult of all developmental transitions, that of self-regeneration, is best mediated within an intimate, one-to-one relationship established with a charismatic other. This person must be someone who is knowledgeable about individual and interpersonal psychodynamics, not be readily thrown off balance by the rapid shifts in consciousness that are induced by structural kinds of regression, and not shy away from the unpleasant content that deep regressions are likely to generate.

How well one is be able to mediate the second type of transition, the external transition, is determined by how well one can grieve the physical and symbolic losses that she or he has sustained within the context of a group composed of like-minded individuals who have been exposed to the same or a similar catastrophic event. For instance, the singing of patriotic songs that possess the power to touch most Americans played a critical role in this nation's capacity to publicly acknowledge and mourn its collective losses immediately following the events of September 11, 2001 (Gusman et. al, 1996; Rosenblatt, Walsh, & Jackson, 1976).

The creative arts therapies field is a professional field that is devoted to the application of art-making as a healing process. This process helps to facilitate clients' contact with objects that hold special emotional resonance and meaning for them. From the perspective of the developmental-relational arts-based model introduced in this book, healing can be defined as the successful negotiation of difficult developmental and external life transitions through an experiential art-making process that improves the quality of a client's sense of self-effectance, mastery, empathy, and relatedness to others (Dosamantes-Beaudry, 1998; Katz, 1982). Because the conceptual framework adopted in this model is founded upon concepts derived from contemporary Western academic disciplines, it is applicable

to persons who live during contemporary times, have been reared in Western societies, and lead modernist lifestyles.

The developmental-relational arts-based model of healing presented
here views creativity to be a positive regenerative response to a state of
cognitive dissonance generated by the experience of emotional crisis. Our
potential to be creative is situated within two kinds of psychosocial spheres,
intimate and public. The intimate sphere is where we forge meaningful
identifications and attachments with those we care most about. It is also
the site where our capacity for illusion making originates and blossoms
during early childhood (Winnicott, 1982). The public sphere is where we
forge meaningful affiliations and identifications with members of various
cultural groups to which we belong. It is also the site where we create
cultural art symbols that can be shared and constructed collaboratively
with others.

Although all arts practitioners cited in this book address these psychosocial spheres in their healing work, creative arts therapists who work with
clients who are facing the transition of self-reconstruction, which involves
structural kinds of regression and deep kinds of self-transformations, are
more likely to emphasize the intimate sphere of psychosocial relationships
and to conduct one-to-one individual sessions that pay detailed attention
to each client's developmental life experiences, psychodynamics, and internal symbolic life. In contrast, arts practitioners who work primarily
with members of groups who are confronting difficult kinds of external
transitions (e.g., terrorist attacks or various forms of social oppression) are
more likely to focus on the interpersonal or the public psychosocial relationships that members forge and maintain with one another and the
expressive or actual art objects they produce in collaboration with one
another.

Although creative artists and artists cited in this book share a healing
intention in the art-making groups they conduct, each individual practitioner is also influenced and motivated by other factors that exert a major
influence upon the kinds of practices that they conduct. These factors
include their own personal and cultural histories, the training they have
received in the arts and in psychotherapy, the way they construe the art-
making process, the various unconscious and conscious personal and social motives that guide their actions, and the kinds of rewards (financial
and psychological) that they receive for their work or services. These factors set into motion subtle, complex behavioral consequences for practitioners that they must grapple with and accommodate to in their work.

For instance, when trained creative arts therapists engage in an art-
making process, they do so with the explicit purpose of achieving particular healing objectives with each client. Many creative arts therapists are
"wounded healers" who have undergone healing journeys of their own
(Halifax, 1982). The artworks that their clients might produce are gener-

ally not intended for public display or consumption but are considered to be private representations of each client's internal symbolic life that can be used by the client or the therapist as a useful source of information in their collaborative therapeutic work together. Although some creative arts therapists are paid directly by clients who seek their healing services, others are reimbursed by health agencies or health care insurance companies. When creative arts therapists are not paid directly for their services by their clients, they are sometimes faced with the difficult moral dilemma of having dual allegiances, which at times may be at odds with the best interests of their clients. Under all circumstances, creative arts therapists are legally bound to protect their clients' rights of confidentiality. They can also be held legally accountable by their clients for the quality of services that they render.

In contrast, trained artists are likely to view the production of a significant artwork to be a major objective of their group art-making process. This process may or may not produce healing effects among the collaborators who become involved in the production of group artwork for a variety of reasons. The artworks produced by artists are meant to be publicly shared with a larger audience. Artists may be financially self-supportive or they may be paid by the private or government agencies that commission their artwork. In the latter instance, they are frequently pressed to meet the political agendas of these agencies. A major source of pressure and status for artists who become involved with the professional art world are the reviews that their artworks receive from art critics.

Negotiating Difficult Developmental Transitions

Within the context of the intimate sphere of a one-to-one relationship established with a creative arts therapist, persons who become involved in an art-making process to heal themselves become engaged in the most difficult developmental transition of all, that of self-regeneration or self-reconstruction, which involves a client's engagement in three kinds of self-object relationships:

1. The first is the subjective relationship that clients establish with the illusory objects that they derive from their own experience or imagination. By forming an emotional attachment and an identification with these illusory objects, and by forming an identification and engaging in pretend playing with them through a preferred art medium, clients gain a concrete, sensory, and imagistic sense of the meaning that these objects hold for them in the present.

2. The second is the intersubjective relationship that clients co-create with their therapist. This type of selfobject relationship provides clients with a functional role model for certain self-psychological functions they need to acquire to function more effectively in the outside world, but which they lack at the outset of

therapy. The cognitive process of transmuting internalization that proceeds from deferred imitation to internalization positively influences a client's overall sense of self-effectance (Kohut, 1984).

3. The third is interpersonal relationship that clients establish with their therapist and with others outside of the therapeutic arena. This relationship provides feedback to clients about how their character and behavior are perceived by others. This relationship fulfills the function of a social conscience, making apparent glaring discrepancies that exist between clients' own self-perceptions and the perceptions that others have about them. This relationship provides clients with an opportunity to consider the kinds of accommodations they might need to make to meet the social expectations of others.

The negotiation of developmental transitions that involve difficult life cycle changes is made more difficult when a client has formed ambivalent, avoidant, or disturbed attachments early in life with significant others (Krueger, 1989; Main, 2000). Children who have been reared by overly intrusive, unavailable, abusive, or neglectful caregivers tend to resort to such defenses as dissociation, splitting, depersonalization, withdrawal, and numbing to protect themselves against further pain by creating a stimulus barrier. Unfortunately, these defenses also tend to distort their perceptions and to foreclose the possibility of forming more mutually gratifying, intimate relationships with others (Krueger, 1989). Children who have experienced persistent abusive parenting styles while growing up face the paradoxical dilemma of being terrified of the very persons upon whom they must rely for their care, safety, and guidance. Therefore, it is not surprising that as these children mature, they are more prone to experience self-fragmentation and involuntary regressions, particularly when they have to cope with overwhelming crisis situations over which they have little control.

Within a creative arts therapies context, clients who become engaged in negotiating difficult developmental transitions have an opportunity to make direct contact with objects and symbols that emerge from their experience or imagination that pertain to early faulty attachments and relationships. As they begin to integrate unmetabolized aspects of these relationships into their self-structure, they simultaneously begin to revise their self-narrative.

The successful negotiation of all difficult developmental transitions requires that clients be able to forge an intense intersubjective relationship with a "wise" adult who can act as a sounding board, serve as a role model for needed psychological functions, and offer the kinds of emotional containment and support that clients need to successfully negotiate the difficult journey of regression-reintegration (Koestler, 1977). This person must be someone who is not only familiar with the healing practices of the client's culture, but also who has the client's best interests in mind, is not intimidated by altered states of consciousness, and is able to help the client work through the derivation of the psychological and symbolic meaning of his or her altered state experience (Barnes and Berke, 1991; Laing, 1967, 1969).

The drama therapy groups that Craig Haen and Kenneth Brannon (2002) conducted with latency-aged boys who shared personal histories of parental abuse, neglect, and abandonment illustrate the ease with which these boys were able to identify with the fantasy characters of superhero, monster, and baby. Within the safe potential space created by their therapists, these boys were able to revisit their experience with early flawed parental relationships by enacting their vulnerability to others, by expressing their fears of abandonment and rejection, and by reconciling their ambivalent emotional reactions toward others. A dramatic role-playing process enabled these boys to better regulate their emotions and to make their fragmented self-experience more coherent.

The successful negotiation of difficult developmental transitions entails the completion of three phases:

1. The first phase is centered around the establishment of a safe potential space, where illusion making can begin to take place. The cases of the three Marys cited in chapter 2 illustrate how, when therapists respond in ways that are congruent with the regressed state and mode of expression of a particular client, and when clients are accorded dignity and respect by being given the opportunity to determine their own destiny, it becomes possible for clients to break through their hard-won isolation, begin to develop an emotional relationship with another human being who shows genuine concern for them, and become engaged in illusion making.

2. The second phase begins when clients feel free to enter the realm of illusion making and begin to create two kinds of selfobject relationships, the subjective relationship they create with an object derived from their own experience or imagination, and the intersubjective relationship they create with their therapist. The spontaneous pretend playing that adults engage in with the illusory objects that they create during the second phase of an art-making healing process makes it possible for them to entertain novel solutions to the problematic situations in which they find themselves. The intimate one-to-one intersubjective relationship that clients establish with their therapist facilitates their internalization of functional aspects of their therapist that they need to form more benign and compassionate kinds of identifications and attachment styles.

   Chapter 4 cited several examples of selfobject relationships that were created by creative arts therapies clients. The sculpture *Never Ending Journey* was created from objects found in an empty lot by a resident of a homeless shelter for women who became involved in creating her own sculpture for the community sculpture park project that was conducted by art therapist Jean Davis (1999). As this woman began to give form to her sculpture, she simultaneously began to construct a more coherent sense of herself. The portrait *John's World*, which was created by an adolescent boy who suffered from cystic fibrosis, was drawn by him to leave a trace of his existence upon this earth during a session he had with his art therapist, Janette Farrell Fenton (2000), a short time before he passed away. The rage-pain dance created by Emily in her dance/movement therapy sessions symbolized for her a persistent traumatic event that she had experienced with her mother before she learned to speak.

When clients create illusory selfobject relationships with objects that they are emotionally drawn to, they create an experiential, concrete, embodied reunion with these objects and, as a result, they develop a richer, more differentiated and complex relationship with them. Similarly, when clients form a positive emotional attachment and identification with their therapist, they begin to actually emulate certain psychological functions that they previously lacked, in social contexts that are outside of the therapeutic arena. Therapists who are treated by their clients as selfobjects provide them with a behavioral template for various ways to treat themselves and others with greater care and compassion.

Once clients form a secure attachment and an identification with illusory objects that hold a special interest for them, and form a reliable intersubjective relationship with their therapist, they can begin to delve more deeply into the symbolic meaning these illusory objects hold for them.

3. The third phase involves a working-through process that leads to the derivation of the personal meaning of the selfobject relationships clients have created and explored during the second phase of the transition process. In this final phase, clients begin to reclaim and to integrate into their self-structure those aspects of themselves that they previously disavowed in themselves and projected onto others.

As clients begin to reorganize their self-experience and to assimilate denied aspects of their self-experience, they begin to develop a more tolerant self-narrative and to acquire the capacity to regulate disruptive emotions more effectively. By internalizing functional aspects of their therapist, clients gain a greater sense of self-effectance which enables them to respond more flexibly and spontaneously to crisis situations. They also are better able to create mutually rewarding intimate relationships with those they care about (Dosamantes-Beaudry, 2001, 2002; Knafo, 2002).

During the third phase, the issue of separation also begins to emerge, providing clients with an opportunity to grieve past and current losses. When clients are able to acknowledge the gift that they have received from their therapist, they are also able to experience a sense of gratitude toward others. For clients for whom abandonment has been a major issue in their lives, this can be a particularly difficult phase to negotiate. As the need for the illusory relationship that clients initially forged with their therapist vanishes, clients begin to perceive their therapist as a real person with her or his own unique set of needs and sense of agency.

The cases of Helen and Irene cited in chapter 4 illustrate the beneficial effects that accrue from being able to reclaim shadow aspects of one's self-experience. Within the safe potential space provided by a creative arts therapist, both of these women were able to integrate and to assimilate into their self-experience aspects of themselves that previously had repelled them. By reclaiming these disavowed aspects of themselves, each was able to detoxify the negative relationships they had developed earlier with significant others in their lives, and to transform the meaning that these relationships held for them in the present.

The length of time that the negotiation of a difficult developmental transition process takes depends upon several factors, including the kinds and quality of attachments the person formed early in life, the level of self-other emotional differentiation the person has achieved, and the severity and depth of trauma that she or he has experienced.

Negotiating Difficult External or Situational Transitions

Even persons who have been able to develop relatively secure attachments with significant others in their lives and who have acquired a relatively stable sense of themselves may become overwhelmed when they are confronted with sudden difficult external events that impose unexpected catastrophic changes over which they have little control and which temporarily thrust them into an involuntary state of regression. External or situational transitions that involve violence and the loss of life can be particularly devastating and can evoke or trigger an involuntary type of regression.

The art-making process involved in the negotiation of difficult external transitions is best carried out within the context of the public sphere, where kindred spirits can gather together to share the experience of having been exposed to the same or a similar catastrophic event, express their unspeakable emotions and ideas, and receive emotional and cognitive support from one another. The negotiation of difficult external transitions can be brief or long, depending upon the emotional history and resilience of each group member and the severity of the trauma that he or she has experienced.

The case of Crystal cited in chapter 4 provides an example of a person who moved through all three phases of a transition process that involved both external and developmental traumatic changes within the context of a long-term dance/movement therapy group. When Crystal was unexpectedly raped and abducted by a neighbor whom she knew, she was shocked by the sudden and violent nature of her attack and was simultaneously temporarily thrusted back to an earlier time in her life, toddlerhood, a time when she had relied upon her security blanket for solace and to maintain her sense of security. The healing process that she underwent during the course of one year showed how, with the unconditional support extended by members of her dance/movement therapy group, she was able to successfully grieve the emotional death that she had experienced immediately following her overwhelming ordeal. Being able to grieve and to reclaim her unspeakable emotions and thoughts following her rape and abduction helped to restore Crystal's emotional equilibrium and desire to resume her life again.

The case of Crystal shows that it is possible for a regressed person to reconstitute her sense of self within the context of a healing art-making group. On the surface, her case would appear to contradict the notion that deep self-reconstruction is best achieved within the context of a one-to-one therapeutic relationship. However, it must be pointed out that in Crystal's case, her self-regeneration was made possible only because the creative arts therapist who led the group was trained to attend to the emergent individual and group dynamics, and her group was made up of individuals who were interested in becoming dance therapists and therefore were convinced of the healing benefits that an art-making process could effect. Also, each member of the group was willing to forego her time in the limelight to devote the entire group's attention for an entire year to the healing process of one of its members. When such conditions abide, it then becomes possible for a structurally regressed person to undergo the process of regression-reintegration that makes self-regeneration possible, within the context of an arts-based healing group.

Because the cataclysmic events of September 11, 2001, suddenly transformed American soil into an unpredictable and potentially hostile place to be, many people who witnessed this event firsthand or even second-hand, through various news media, and who were able to identify with the victims of the catastrophe, were deeply emotionally shaken. Violent catastrophic events shatter one's faith in the trustworthiness of people. They compel normal people to respond to abnormal situations (Lahad, 1999).

Confronted with the assassination of their leader Yitzhak Rabin in 1995, many youth from Tel Aviv gathered at their city's public square and transformed this public space into a site for communal mourning and remembrance (Klingman, Shalev, & Pearlman, 2000). Through the graffiti peace symbols that they spontaneously scrolled on the walls of their city's public square, these young people were able to symbolize their refusal to allow their dreams for peace and a future world to be obliterated. Following the catastrophic events of September 11, 2001, the buildings at the periphery of ground zero in downtown Manhattan were plastered with the improvised memorials created by survivors for those who perished in the disaster. Tributes of gratitude were also dedicated to the courageous firemen, policemen, and other service people whose altruistic acts of bravery helped to restore Americans' collective sense of calm and faith in the goodness of others.

In times of crisis, those who are most directly and intensely affected yearn for a sense of safety and solidarity with kindred spirits who have undergone a similar ordeal (Almond, 1974; Turner, 1969). The public sphere of interpersonal relationships is where mutual support can be obtained, the potential fear of violence can be reduced, and *amistad* (fellowship) can be restored. By joining with others who share a similar worldview and have been exposed to the same cataclysmic event, a terrorized person's sense of isolation, helplessness, and hopelessness can be dispelled.

The encounter group phenomenon that surfaced in this country during the 1960s attracted a wide spectrum of cultural groups from American society because these groups offered participants a place where they could relate to one another openly and honestly as equals without fear of retribution, and could restore their faith in a better world at a time when global chaos and intercultural conflict seemed to prevail (Rogers, 1970). During contemporary times, members of art-making groups that share a healing intention become involved in creating three kinds of object relationships:

1. The first is the interpersonal relationship that group members establish with one another through an expressive arts medium. The subsequent verbal feedback that group members receive about their character or behavior tends to be focused upon their unique interpersonal relational style and upon the kinds of defenses they use to cope with conflict.

2. The second relationship is the subjective relationship that group participants establish with the actual art object that they collaboratively create with other group members. For each group member, this art object represents some significant aspect of his or her own internal symbolic world.

3. Although members of art-making groups enact the intersubjective relationship they have with their therapist or with the artist who directs their group art project, for the most part, this relationship tends to be unconsciously acted out and generally does not receive the kind of systematic attention that it does within the one-to-one relationship that is established with a creative arts therapist (who works personally and individually with a client who is undergoing a deep, structural regression to achieve self-regeneration).

The healing processes facilitated by several creative arts therapists and by two artists who make use of an art-making group process were described in chapter 6. *Spirit Dances 2—The Crones: A Celebration of Life,* performed by master dance performers over the age of 50 years, explored and exalted the creative spirit and wisdom of older women (Scott, 2002). This dance, conceived by Marion Scott, paid homage to the archetype of the crone. Through an honest depiction of the various facets of what it means to live as an older woman in a society that continues to project its misogynist and ageist attitudes upon older women, this dance served as an antidote against these destructive social attitudes. It did so by validating each performer's life experience and by valorizing the socially stigmatized life cycle of senescence that many Western women find they must negotiate alone.

The large-scale public artworks such as *The Great Wall of Los Angeles,* and *La Memoria de Nuestra Tierra Durango,* conceived and produced by Judith F. Baca and her collaborators at SPARC, engaged large numbers of young adults from various ethnic communities in the creation of public artworks to benefit their communities (Baca, 2002). These monumental artworks provided members of marginalized ethnic groups with an opportunity to valorize their cultural identities and cultural histories. *The World Wall* continues to serve as a symbolic source of inspiration for groups who are engaged in dialogue about ways to reduce global conflict and to restore balance in the world (Roth, 1991).

Through their "portable studio," art therapists Debra Kalmanowitz and Bobby Lloyd (1999) attempted to bring comfort and to create a safe healing vessel for those whose lives had been ravaged by war and were forced to live in the refugee war camps of Slovania and Croatia. The crisis intervention groups organized by drama therapist Mooli Lahad (1999) provided the evacuees from Kyriat Schmona with an opportunity to restore their sense of trust and faith in others and to recover their capacity to function adequately in the world again.

Being able to share one's symbolic inner life and to work collaboratively with others in the creation of actual art objects that have symbolic meaning for the group helps group members forge a strong bond of solidarity with one another. The support members receive from the collective allows each to cope better with whatever catastrophic events they do encounter and to express greater concern and compassion for others' circumstances, even toward those who may not share their cultural identities and worldview values.

FUTURE TRENDS IN THE CREATIVE ARTS THERAPIES FIELD

Currently, creative arts therapists are making a significant contribution within settings that provide health, educational, and welfare services to people who are coping with difficult developmental and external transitions, such as schools, hospitals and community welfare facilities, wellness centers, hospices, and international agencies that are devoted to helping people during times of crisis.

The skills of creative arts therapists are being used in schools to promote positive emotional, cognitive, and social changes (Harvey, 1989; Ulfursdottir & Erwin, 1999) and to prevent the outbreak of youth violence and other self-destructive behaviors (Reed, 2002; Slotoroff, 1994). Creative arts therapists are helping children and adolescents with histories of abandonment or abuse who live in residential treatment centers to develop a more positive and coherent sense of themselves (Haen & Brannon, 2002). They are providing alternative effective methods of working with children who have been sexually abused (MacIntosh, in press; Weltman, 1986).

In residential and outpatient psychiatric settings, creative arts therapists are helping adult clients develop a more stable, coherent, and integrated sense of themselves (Schoop & Mitchell, 1974). They work with battered women and women with eating disorders to help them find less self-destructive coping patterns (Krantz, 1989; Leventhal & Chang, 1991). They work in homeless shelters to create a space where displaced or lost persons in urban communities can find a safe place to be (Davis, 1999; Ginzberg, 1991). They use creative alternative methods to help women cope with sexual abuse (Lev-Wiesel, 1998). In hospital and hospice settings, creative arts therapists are working with people who face the prospect of dying by providing them with safe ways to express their concerns and by offering the kind of support that helps to enhance each person's quality of life experience (Dibbell-Hope, 2000; Fenton, 2000; Gunter, 2000; Mendelsohn, 1999; Tsao, Gordon, Maranto, Lerman, & Murasko, 1991). They work in nursing homes to help older adults cope with their sense of isolation and anxiety about dying (Smith, 2000). Creative arts therapists work under the auspices of national and international agencies that provide support for people who have been displaced by the outbreak of man-made catastrophic events. In the field, they help to create a safe vessel within which displaced persons or war refugees can feel free to vent their unexpressed emotions, voice their unspeakable thoughts, and restore their hope for a future tomorrow (Kalmanowitz & Lloyd, 1999; Lahad, 1999).

At a time when our society is facing the prospect of an ever-increasing and persistent state of collective anxiety over the potential outbreak of terrorism in the future, the health, educational, and welfare resources of our nation need to be harnessed to address this major concern. We need to strengthen our understanding of the arts by becoming educated early in life about the valuable contribution the arts can make to the quality of our lives. Our various educational systems can achieve this goal by adopting and implementing various developmental approaches to arts education in their curriculum. The creation of public artworks needs to be encouraged and funded by government and private agencies.

Because the current health care system of the United States is being managed for profit, the responses this system is likely to make in addressing this urgent need are likely to be minimal and limited to brief, crisis intervention, prevention-oriented strategies that third-party service providers find financially viable to implement (Cimons, 1996). As insufficient as these responses are likely to be, they will result in opening up further opportunities for practitioners who offer alternative arts-based approaches to healing. Such approaches are likely to be viewed as being more cost-effective than the psychopharmacological care that is currently being provided by psychiatric units in hospitals. This is a challenge that creative arts therapists and artists who share a healing intention are well positioned to meet because they are already providing a broad spectrum of individual and group healing services at the various health and welfare facilities where they currently work (Dosamantes-Beaudry, 1997; Zwerling, 1989).

As the creative arts therapies field continues to thrive, it will be critical for its survival to establish its own unique hybrid but independent identity as a healing profession while maintaining collaborative working relationships with members of other professional disciplines who share an integrative, holistic approach to healing. The creative arts therapies field needs to find a home of its own and not simply be appendaged to other departments at universities or in professional schools. This is necessary for the field to avoid being marginalized, relegated to a subordinate position, and eliminated when educational funding declines. During times of fiscal retrenchment, department chairs tend to become protective toward their own academic discipline and to view interdisciplinary arts therapies programs as expendable and not essential to the primary mission of their departments. However, because creative arts therapies fill a critical role in the mediation of difficult developmental and external transitions that an increasing number of people in our society are being pressed to confront, they can no longer be discarded with the simple explanation that they are an expendable frill that our society can readily do without.

Independent creative arts therapies departments need to be established that will encompass all of the creative arts therapies (art, dance, drama, music, and poetry) under one roof within universities, professional schools, or medical centers. Such departments will be able to offer courses that are unique to each arts therapy modality, courses that cut across all arts therapies modalities, and courses that connect the creative arts therapies field to other disciplines (arts, social sciences, education, and medicine). As independent departments, creative arts therapies departments will be able to provide a more comprehensive, integrated, and systematic understanding of art-making as a healing process with the potential to help people mediate the difficult developmental and situational challenges they face while living in an increasingly unpredictable, dangerous, and unstable world. For, in the end, the most critical function that our capacity to be creative may serve will be to remind us of the darker side of our nature, so that we may act to restore balance in our intimate as well as in our public lives.

REFERENCES

Almond, R. (1974). *The healing community.* New York: Jason Aronson.

Baca, J. F. (2002, January 14). Birth of a movement #1. *Judith F. Baca Reader, JB Archive,* pp. 1–32.

Barnes, M., & Berke, J. (1991). *Mary Barnes: Two approaches of a journey through madness.* London: Free Association Books.

Cimons, M. (1996, May 19). Gray areas fuel mental health coverage debate. *New York Times,* pp. A1, A16.

Davis, J. (1999). Report: Environmental art therapy-metaphors in the field. *Arts in Psychotherapy Journal, 26* (1), 45–49.

Dibbell-Hope, S. (2000). The use of dance/movement therapy in psychological adaptation to breast cancer. *Arts in Psychotherapy Journal, 27* (1), 51–68.

Dosamantes-Alperson, E. (1979). The intrapsychic and the interpersonal in experiential movement psychotherapy. *American Journal of Dance Therapy, 3,* 20–31.

Dosamantes-Beaudry, I. (1997). Reconfiguring identity. *Arts in Psychotherapy Journal, 24* (1), 51–57.

Dosamantes-Beaudry, I. (1998). Regression-reintegration: Central psychodynamic principle in rituals of transition. *Arts in Psychotherapy Journal, 25* (2), 79–84.

Dosamantes-Beaudry, I. (2001). Frida Kahlo: Self-other representation and self healing through art. *Arts in Psychotherapy Journal, 28* (1), 5–17.

Dosamantes-Beaudry, I. (2002). Frida Kahlo: The creation of a cultural icon. *Arts in Psychotherapy Journal, 29* (1), 3–12.

Erikson, E. H. (1968). *Identity, youth and crisis.* New York: Norton.

Fenton, J. F. (2000). Cystic fibrosis and art therapy. *Arts in Psychotherapy Journal, 27* (1), 15–25.

Ginzberg, J. (1991). In search of a voice: Working with homeless men. *American Journal of Dance Therapy, 13* (1), 33–48.

Gunter, M. (2000). Art therapy as an intervention to stabilize the defense of children undergoing bone marrow transplantation. *Arts in Psychotherapy Journal, 27* (1), 3–14.

Gusman, F. D., Stewart, J., Hiley Young, B., Riney, S. J., Abueg, F. R., & Blake, D. D. (1996). A multicultural developmental approach to treating trauma. In A. J. Marsella, M. J. Friedman, E. T. Gerrity, & R. M. Scurfield (Eds.), *Ethnocultural aspects of posttraumatic stress disorders* (pp. 439–459). Washington, DC: American Psychological Association.

Haen, C. & Brannon, K. H. (2002). Superheroes, monsters and babies: Roles of strength, destruction and vulnerability for emotionally disturbed boys. *Arts in Psychotherapy Journal, 29* (1), 31–40.

Halifax, J. (1982). *Shaman the wounded healer.* New York: Crossroad.

Harvey, S. (1989). Creative arts therapies in the classroom: A study of cognitive, emotional and motivational changes. *American Journal of Dance Therapy, 11* (2), 85–100.

Kalmanowitz, D., & Lloyd, B. (1999). Fragments of art at work: Art therapy in the former Yugoslavia. *Arts in Psychotherapy Journal, 26* (1), 15–25.

Katz, E. (1982). *Boiling energy.* Cambridge, MA: Harvard University Press.

Klingman, A., Shalev, R., & Pearlman, A. (2000). Graffiti: A creative means of youth coping with collective trauma. *Arts in Psychotherapy Journal, 27* (5), 299–307.

Knafo, D. (2002). Revisiting Kris's concept of regression in the service of the ego in art. *Psychoanalytic Psychology, 19* (1), 24–29.

Koestler, A. (1977). In W. Anderson (Ed.), *Therapy and the arts* (pp. 3–10). New York: Harper & Row.

Kohut, H. (1984). *How does analysis cure?* Chicago: University of Chicago Press.

Krantz, A. M. (1989). Growing into her body: Dance/movement therapy for women with eating disorders. *American Journal of Dance Therapy, 21* (2), 81–103.

Krueger, D. W. (1989). *Body self and psychological self.* New York: Brunner/Mazel.

Lahad, M. (1999). The use of drama therapy with crisis intervention groups, following mass evacuation. *Arts in Psychotherapy Journal, 26* (1), 27–33.

Laing, R. D. (1967). *The politics of experience.* New York: Ballantine Books.

Laing, R. D. (1969). *The politics of the family and other essays.* New York: Random House.

Leventhal, F., & Chang, M. (1991). Dance/movement therapy with battered women: A paradigm of action. *American Journal of Dance Therapy, 13* (2), 131–145.

Lev-Wiesel, R. (1998). Use of drawing technique to encourage verbalization in adult survivor of sexual abuse. *Arts in Psychotherapy Journal, 25* (4), 257–262.

MacIntosh, H. (in press). Sounds of healing: Music in group work with survivors of sexual abuse. *Arts in Psychotherapy Journal.*

Main, M. (2000). The categories of infant, child and adult attachment. Flexible vs. inflexible attention under attachment related stress. *Journal of American Psychoanalytic Association, 48,* 1055–1096.

Mendelsohn, J. (1999). Dance/movement therapy with hospitalized children. *American Journal of Dance Therapy, 21* (2), 65–80.

Reed, I. (2002, May 6). Heritage mural "reCollections" installed at Durango Arts Center. *Four Corners Business Journal,* pp. 1–3.

Rogers, C. (1970). *On encounter groups.* New York: Harper & Row.

Rosenblatt, P. C., Walsh, R. P. & Jackson, D. A. (1976). *Grief and mourning in cross-cultural perspective.* New Haven, CT: H.R.A.F. Press.

Roth, M. (1991, November 14). Towards a world in balance. A conversation with Judy Baca: Part I. *Artweek,* pp. 10–11.

Schoop, T., & Mitchell, P. (1974). *Won't you join the dance?* Palo Alto, CA: National Press Books.

Scott, M. (2002, March 7). Personal communication. Los Angeles: CA.

Slotoroff, C. (1994). Drumming technique for assertiveness and anger management in the short-term psychiatric setting for adult and adolescent survivors of trauma. *Music Therapy Perspectives, 12,* 111–116.

Smith, A. G. (2000). Exploring death anxiety with older adults through developmental transformations. *Arts in Psychotherapy Journal, 27* (5), 321–331.

Tsao, C., Gordon, T. Maranto, C., Lerman, C., & Murasko, D. (1991). The effects of music and biological imagery on immune response. In C. D. Maranto (Ed.), *Applications of music in medicine* (pp. 85–121). Washington, DC: National Association for Music Therapy.

Turner, V. W. (1969). *The ritual process.* Chicago: Aldine.

Ulfursdottir, L. O., & Erwim, P. G. (1999). The influence of music on social cognitive skills. *Arts in Psychotherapy Journal, 26* (2), 81–84.

Weltman, M. (1986). Movement therapy with children who have been sexually abused. *American Journal of Dance Therapy, 9,* 47–66.

Winnicott, D. D. (1982). *Playing and reality.* New York: Penguin Books.

Zwerling, I. (1989). The creative arts therapies as "real therapies." *American Journal of Dance Therapy, 11* (1), 19–38.

Author Index

Subject Index

About the Author

IRMA DOSAMANTES-BEAUDRY is Professor in the World Arts and Cultures Department at the University of California, Los Angeles. She conducts Intensive Dance/Movement Therapy workshops internationally, and is Editor-in-Chief of the international *Arts in Psychotherapy Journal.*